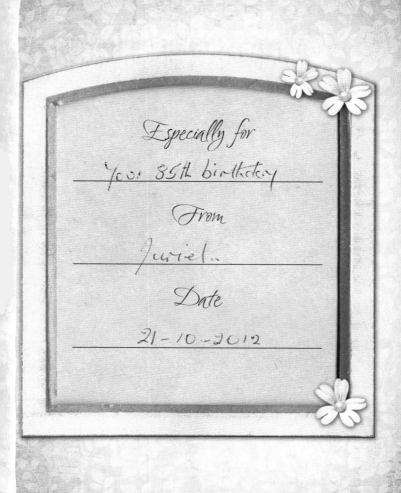

Especially for

You: 85th birthday

From

Juriel..

Date

21–10–2012

Circle of Friends Ministries
Connected in Faith

Shared Encouragement

Inspiration for a Woman's Soul

BARBOUR

Circle of Friends is a ministry of women helping women. Born out of a small accountability group that led to a women's Bible study, Circle of Friends Ministries is now a nonprofit organization dedicated to encouraging women to find and follow Christ. Our desire is to encourage one another to love God more deeply and to follow Him with a heart of passion that reaches out and draws others along with us on our journey.

"Circle of Friends are women of biblical depth and compassion for others. They have a knack for bringing humor, hope, and practical application to everyday situations."

—CAROL KENT, SPEAKER AND AUTHOR
When I Lay My Isaac Down
and *A New Kind of Normal*

"Circle of Friends has its finger on the pulse of the heart-needs of women today. Through word and song they link arms with women around the globe to bring the hope and healing of Jesus Christ."

—SHARON JAYNES, SPEAKER AND AUTHOR
Becoming a Woman Who Listens to God
and *Extraordinary Moments with God*

ISBN 978-1-61626-203-7

Our mission is to publish and distribute inspirational products offering exceptional value and biblical encouragement to the masses.

Member of the
Evangelical Christian
Publishers Association

Printed in India.

Introduction

Who can understand the heart of a woman—with all its joys and triumphs, challenges and heartaches—better than another woman? We are told in the book of Titus that mature women of the faith are able to be "teachers of good things" and in Hebrews that we are to "exhort [encourage] one another daily."

Shared Encouragement is a devotional written by women who have a passion and love for Jesus. Their stories, insights, biblical applications, and refreshing honesty in everyday trials in their lives will encourage your heart and strengthen your faith. So grab a cup of coffee or tea, pull up a chair, and share life, share encouragement, with your "Circle of Friends." You'll laugh, you'll cry, you'll find that you have truly found a place to belong. . . .

Mountain Ranges

God is our refuge and strength,
an ever-present help in trouble.
PSALM 46:1 NIV

Do you see clearly? Are you able to view things from under the fog you are in? I have been in that place far more often than I would like to admit. Things discourage me and cause me to want to give up and walk away. Sometimes I feel as though all I ever do is walk over that same mountain range day in and day out. It feels like I will never get to the end and walk on flat land again.

Have you ever been that discouraged? Admit it! Be honest.

This morning when I woke up after yet another trip across that mountain range, I received this scripture from one of my sons. He sent it to me in a very simple e-mail. Then he said,

"I love you." Amazing how those three little words can speak volumes. I received them from my son, but as I write this, I realize that they were from God! The above scripture is the reference my son sent. He knows me well. He knows that when my heart is fearful, when I am feeling overwhelmed, I need to be reminded that God is with me and that I will not fall. That He will help me at the break of day. Yes, my friends, God is there; and more than that, He loves you!

BECKI REISER
Circle of Friends

God's Blueprint
for This Moment

"So don't worry about tomorrow,
for tomorrow will bring its own worries.
Today's trouble is enough for today."
MATTHEW 6:34 NLT

The battle always has to be fought before the victory is won, though many people think they must have the victory *before* the battle. The conflict with worry and fear is almost always there—each person must overcome or be overcome. But we must fight each battle of our lives in the strength of Jesus' victory. He said, "As the Father has sent me, I am sending you" (John 20:21 NIV). We are to be like Jesus—One of whom Satan is afraid!

When we worry, we are carrying tomorrow's load with today's strength; carrying two days in one. We are moving into tomorrow ahead of time. There is just one day in the calendar of action—today. The Holy Spirit does not give a clear blueprint of our whole lives, but only of the moments, one by one.

We all have the same enemies—we are all preyed upon by frustration and worry. In India, Australia, Japan, Germany—we need the same Holy Spirit. We need to remember that we are children of God, living within His constant care. God knows and is interested both in the hardest problems we face and the tiniest details that concern us. He knows how to put everything in place, like a jigsaw puzzle, to make a beautiful picture.

CORRIE TEN BOOM
He Cares for You

Without a Doubt

"I have loved you with an everlasting love."
JEREMIAH 31:3 NIV

I remember once seeing the indignation of a mother I knew, stirred to its very depths by a little doubting on the part of one of her children. She had brought two little girls to my house to leave them while she did some errands. One of them, with the happy confidence of childhood, abandoned herself to all the pleasures she could find in my nursery and sang and played until her mother's return.

The other one, with the wretched caution and mistrust of maturity, sat down alone in a corner to wonder whether her mother would remember to come back for her, and to fear she would be forgotten, and to imagine her mother would be glad of the chance to get rid of her anyhow, because she was such a naughty girl, and ended with working herself up into a perfect frenzy of despair.

The look on that mother's face, when upon her return the weeping little girl told what was the matter with her, I shall not easily forget. Grief, wounded love, indignation, and pity all strove together for mastery. But indignation gained the day, and I doubt if that little girl was ever so vigorously dealt with before.

A hundred times in my life since has that scene come up before me with deepest teaching and has compelled me, peremptorily, to refuse admittance to the doubts about my heavenly Father's love and care and remembrance of me that have clamored at the door of my heart for entrance.

HANNAH WHITALL SMITH
The Christian's Secret of a Happy Life

The Promise of Joy

Weeping may endure for a night,
but joy cometh in the morning.
PSALM 30:5 KJV

Have you experienced suffering? Perhaps you are hurting even now. Tough times are a reality for all of us.

The psalmist David was well acquainted with hardship. He used phrases such as "the depths," "the pit," and even "the grave" to describe them. Although he was known as a man after God's own heart, at times David was pursued by his enemies and forced to run for his life. He also lived with the consequences of committing murder and adultery, even long after receiving God's forgiveness.

God is faithful, and suffering is temporary. This is a promise we can claim, as David did, when facing difficulty or depression. David

experienced God's faithfulness throughout the ups and downs of his life.

King Solomon, one of the wisest men who ever lived, concludes in the third chapter of Ecclesiastes that there is a time for everything, including "a time to weep and a time to laugh" (v. 4 NIV).

Some trials are short lived. Others are more complex. As believers, we can find joy in the Lord even as certain trials remain a backdrop in our lives. All suffering will end one day when we meet Jesus. The Bible assures us that in heaven there will be no tears.

Your loving heavenly Father has not forgotten you. You may feel that relief will never come, but take courage. It will.

EMILY BIGGERS
Whispers of Wisdom for Busy Women

The Most Beautiful Woman in the World

They saw that his face was radiant.
Then Moses would put the veil back over his
face until he went in to speak with the LORD.
EXODUS 34:35 NIV

Film legend Audrey Hepburn was named the most naturally beautiful woman of all time by a panel of experts in June 2004. Hepburn topped the poll of beauty editors, makeup artists, fashion editors, model agencies, and fashion photographers who were asked to choose their top ten beauties from the list of one hundred compiled on www.smh.com. The women were chosen for their "embodiment of natural beauty, healthy living, *beautiful on the inside and out*, with great skin and a natural glow to their personality, as well as their complexion."

The article went on to say that Hepburn is the personification of natural beauty because "she has a rare charm and *inner beauty* that radiates when she smiles. Her skin looks fresh in all her films and her personality really shines through as someone warm and lively."

Did you notice that Audrey Hepburn's inner beauty was mentioned twice in the judges' reasoning for choosing her? Sure, there were many other beauties who made the list. Some may have been even more beautiful than Hepburn, but apparently their inner beauty was found lacking, even though their exterior beauty was striking.

That's good news, isn't it? That means even if our skin isn't flawless and even if our teeth aren't perfectly straight, we can still "radiate beauty" because of our gorgeous inner looks.

Spend some time with God today, and get a makeover by the Master. Soon you'll radiate His love, and people will find you attractive.

MICHELLE MEDLOCK ADAMS
Secrets of Beauty

The Center of Life

*Six days thou shalt labour, and do all thy
work: but the seventh day
is the sabbath of the LORD thy God:
in it thou shalt not do any work.*
DEUTERONOMY 5:13-14 KJV

Workaholics, beware! Don't expect God to
sanction your seven-day workweek.

God did not mean our jobs to be everyday
things. We wear out emotionally and spiritually
if we focus continually on work. Worse than
that, it quickly becomes our god. When we become too wrapped up in our careers, the place
He is designed for—the center of our lives—
becomes filled with thoughts of how we can
cram more labor into our days, get things done,
and improve our status in the company. Before

long, we're empty and tired. We've been grasping at straws, and suddenly we find a hayrack in our hands, not the success we'd looked for.

Life without God is empty. So take a day of rest, worship God, and get your life in focus. Give God His proper place, and life will go more smoothly. You'll find success, even if it's not in the place you expected it.

Lord, I need to keep You in the center of my life. Help me spend Sunday worshipping You, not focusing on the things I "need" to accomplish.

PAMELA L. McQUADE
Daily Wisdom for the Workplace

Ready to Fly

He brought me out into a spacious place;
he rescued me because he delighted in me.
PSALM 18:19 NIV

*M*any of us live busy, lonely lives. We can be
surrounded by people, even family, and still
feel isolated and alone. It's risky to be known.
What if in a moment of finally stepping out of
our cocoon, ready to spread our wings and fly,
someone laughs at us—or worse still, simply
turns her back and continues with her conversation? When a child is born and the very first
face she focuses on is the face of her adoring
mother, part of the rip of Eden is healed. When
that love and acceptance are further strengthened through the years by her father, and by
family and friends, it will be hard to convince
this little one that she is not worth loving. The
trouble with the human experience of many is

that the love they needed and craved as a child was withheld, and the tear of separation that began in Eden has gotten bigger. One of the greatest spiritual gifts of rebirth when we give our lives to Christ is that we have fresh eyes to look into and see how much we are treasured. You have a Father who adores you, who delights in your laugh, who celebrates your gifts, and who catches every tear that falls from your eyes. His love will give you the courage to leave the cocoon behind and fly.

SHEILA WALSH
Let Go

Listen and Reflect

As often as possible Jesus withdrew to out-of-the-way places for prayer.
LUKE 5:16 MSG

The time is short. Listen carefully to My words. Hide them in your heart, for they need a time for developing within you, even as seeds that are planted in the earth. My word needs a period to rest quietly within your heart until it is quickened by the Spirit. Then shall it rise in newness of life. In this way I will bring forth through you new truth and fresh revelation.

No new truth can be generated in the midst of activity. New life springs from the placid pools of reflection. Quiet meditation and deep worship are a prerequisite if you are to receive My words and comprehend My thoughts.

Some graces of the soul are gained in motion. Faith may be developed in action, endurance in the midst of storms and turmoil. Courage may come in the front lines of battle. But wisdom and understanding and revelation unfold as dew forms on the petals of a rose—in quietness.

Did not Jesus learn from His Father through the silences of lonely nights on the mountain? Shall I not teach you likewise? Will you, My child, set aside unto Me these hours for lonely vigil that I may have opportunity to minister to you?

FRANCES J. ROBERTS
Progress of Another Pilgrim

Fearfully and Wonderfully Made

For you created my inmost being;
you knit me together in my mother's womb.
I praise you because I am fearfully and
wonderfully made; your works are
wonderful, I know that full well.
PSALM 139:13–14 NIV

$\mathcal{I}$ do think God wants us to take reasonable care of our bodies. After all, it is the only living sacrifice we have to offer Him, and the scripture does say physical training is beneficial (Romans 12:1; 1 Corinthians 9:24–27; and 1 Timothy 4:8). But the obsessive pursuit of perfection is not reasonable—and it will never bring us the love we desire.

At the end of the day it's not beauty and physical fitness that we really want. What we really want is someone to love us. And we think that means we have to make ourselves lovable. But love isn't love if you have to earn it. Real love—God's love—is unconditional. He even loves women with cellulite. In fact, His Word says we are fearfully and wonderfully made, just the way we are. We don't need to change a thing to be lovable.

I think what God wanted to say to me—and what I was finally able to hear once He had my undivided attention—is that there are different kinds of love. And I was pursuing the wrong kind. Around this time, my children and I were sitting on the couch one evening. Tara looked up from my lap and said, "Mommy, you're the bestest pillow in the world." I don't think she could have said that with as much conviction to a thin-thighed mommy.

Donna Partow
This Isn't the Life I Signed Up For

He Enjoys You

*The LORD your God is in your midst,
a mighty one who will save; he will rejoice over
you with gladness; he will quiet you by his love;
he will exult over you with loud singing.*

ZEPHANIAH 3:17 ESV

Memory is a powerful part of each one of us. Perhaps you can see your father cheering you on in a sports event, or you remember your mother stroking your feverish forehead while you lay sick in bed. With those mental pictures comes a recollection of emotion—how good it felt to be cheered and encouraged—how comforting it was to be loved and attended.

Zephaniah's words remind us that God is our loving parent. Our mighty Savior offers us a personal relationship, loving and rejoicing over us, His children, glad that we live and move in Him. He is the Lord of the universe, and yet

He will quiet our restless hearts and minds with His tender love. He delights in our lives and celebrates our union with Him. We can rest in His affirmation and love, no matter what circumstances surround us.

LEAH SLAWSON
Daily Encouragement for Single Women

Seeking to Please Jesus

Then the servant girl who kept the door said to Peter, "You are not also one of this Man's disciples, are you?" He said, "I am not."
JOHN 18:17 NKJV

For three years Peter publicly followed Jesus. The disciple stood near the Master during the miracles, the messages, and all the good times. Everyone could see him sticking by Jesus.

But when Jesus came before the high priest, His life in danger, Peter caved in to fear and denied his Lord to a simple servant girl. Why would he care what a slave thought? Perhaps he feared that word of his presence would get back to the ruling priests.

Like Peter, we've caved in because of what others we barely knew thought of us. Instead of obeying the Lord we've loved, we've sought approval of both people who barely matter and those who could have some earthly authority over us. In a split second, love for the all-powerful Lord hardly seemed to matter.

Instead of allowing fear to rule our lives, we need to steadfastly rest in Jesus' love. He who holds the entire world in His hands can direct our lives in the face of bad opinions from those who think ill of us. When we're faithful to Him, we hold firm to the One who really matters.

Lord, I want to hold on to You and please You only. Give me strength to do what I cannot do under my own power.

PAMELA L. MCQUADE
Daily Wisdom for the Workplace

Fruit for the Picking

Early in the morning, as Jesus was on his way back to the city, he was hungry. Seeing a fig tree by the road, he went up to it but found nothing on it except leaves. Then he said to it, "May you never bear fruit again!" Immediately the tree withered.
MATTHEW 21:18–19 NIV

Everything in nature is designed to grow, to produce fruit. Jesus cursed a fig tree once for giving the illusion of having fruit to offer. It was in full bloom but bore no figs. He commanded it to wither and die (Matthew 21:18–19). It was useless, taking up space and pretending to be something that it was not.

Some people are like this fig tree. They walk through life appearing to have a lot to offer, but up close, you find great pretenders. They bear no "fruit"—have nothing useful to give others—

they're all show and no substance. A lack of productivity and the refusal to mature will stymie a life that is working—and it won't work for long.

God wants us moving forward, being productive, maturing from the challenges we face. We then have "fruit" to share—the life lessons we pick up along the way. When we pass on these lessons, we empower others to grow and be fruitful as well. This is the cycle of life. We cross-pollinate!

MICHELLE MCKINNEY HAMMOND
How to Make Life Work

Above the Clouds

"I, even I, am he who comforts you."
ISAIAH 51:12 NIV

Every time I take off in an airplane on a gray, dreary, rainy day, I'm always amazed at how we can fly right up through the dark, wet clouds, so thick that we can't see one thing out the window, and then suddenly rise above it all and have the ability to see for miles. Up there the sky is sunny, clear, and blue. I keep forgetting that no matter how bad the weather gets, it's possible to rise above the storm to a place where everything is fine.

Our spiritual and emotional lives are much the same. When the dark clouds of trial, struggle, grief, or suffering roll in and settle on us so thick that we can barely see ahead of us, it's easy to forget there is a place of calm, light, clarity, and peace we can rise to. If we take God's hand

in those difficult times, He will lift us up above our circumstances to the place of comfort, warmth, and safety He has for us.

One of my favorite names for the Holy Spirit is the Comforter (John 14:26 KJV). Just as we don't have to beg the sun for light, we don't have to beg the Holy Spirit for comfort either. He *is* comfort.

STORMIE OMARTIAN
The Power of a Praying Woman

Contagious Laughter

And Sarah said, "God has made me laugh,
and all who hear will laugh with me."
GENESIS 21:6 NKJV

Nothing brings more joy to our hearts than when God blesses our lives. Like Sarah, we may at first laugh with disbelief when God promises us our heart's desire. For some reason, we doubt that He can do what we deem impossible. Yet God asks us, as He did Sarah, "Is anything too hard for the LORD?" (Genesis 18:14 NKJV).

Then when the blessings shower down upon us, we overflow with joy. Everything seems bright and right with the world. With God, the impossible has become a reality. We bubble over with laughter, and when we laugh, the world laughs with us! It's contagious!

When Satan bombards us with lies—"God's not real"; "You'll never get that job"; "Mr. Right?

He'll never come along"—it's time to look back at God's Word and remember Sarah. Imbed in your mind the truth that with God, nothing is impossible (see Matthew 19:26). And then, in the midst of the storm, in the darkness of night, in the crux of the trial, laugh, letting the joy of God's truth be your strength.

DONNA K. MALTESE
Whispers of Wisdom for Busy Women

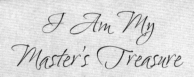

I Am My Master's Treasure

"Look at the birds of the air,
that they do not sow,
nor reap nor gather into barns,
and yet your heavenly Father feeds them.
Are you not worth much more than they?"
MATTHEW 6:26 NASB

The opal is a beautiful stone, but when it lies in a jeweler's case, it's cold and lusterless, with no life in it. But let the jeweler pick it up in his hand and the warmth of his touch brings out the brilliant hues and colors. Likewise, when we hold the Lord at arm's length and refuse to let Him work in our lives, there is no brilliance, no color, no depth to living. But when we allow the touch of the Master's hand, His love warms us and we know we are jewels for His kingdom. Until then we are hidden treasures.

You may have seen the picture of the little boy saying, "I know I'm SOMEBODY. . . 'cause GOD don't make no JUNK!" That little boy has a better understanding of God's love and forgiveness than many adult parents do. Their self-esteem has been destroyed because of something that's gone wrong in the family. Guilt has destroyed their self-esteem, and they feel worthless. I know that feeling—I felt it for eleven months without relief, and I still feel it occasionally when I momentarily forget I am very special to God.

BARBARA JOHNSON
The Best of Barbara Johnson

Rewiring My Buttons

*Now that you have purified yourselves
by obeying the truth so that you have sincere
love for each other, love one another
deeply, from the heart.*
1 Peter 1:22 niv

Do you ever feel like you could be just a
dandy Christian if it weren't for other *people*?
Sometimes I feel like I could shower love and
goodwill all around me until someone goes and
pushes my buttons. When conflict raises its ugly
head, watch out! The un-Christian thoughts
that sometimes run through my head are not
glorifying to my Lord and Savior.

And yet God put me into a world where
I have to interact with other people—even
people who sometimes cause me to get a little
grumpy, even downright mad. Jesus dealt with
these kinds of people all the time. They were

always trying to push His buttons and make Him say or do something wrong. The neat thing is that they never could. Jesus didn't have any buttons that made Him say or do mean things. He was perfect. I wish I were more like Him and didn't have those buttons. But, because I am a sinful creature, I do. And I need to rewire them so that when my buttons are pushed, I react with patience and love instead of frustration and anger, just like Jesus reacted. Surely I could follow the example of my Lord and Savior whom I claim to love and follow. Who, I know for a fact, puts up with some very annoying behaviors from me and constantly forgives me.

I think it's time to do some rewiring.

JANINE MILLER
Circle of Friends

Unmerited Love

God shows his love for us in that while we were still sinners, Christ died for us.
ROMANS 5:8 ESV

The truth is, God *does* love us. Whether or not we feel loved, regardless of what we have done or where we have come from, He loves us with an infinite, incomprehensible love.

God loves me—not because I have loved Him since I was four years old, not because I seek to please Him, not because I speak at conferences and write books. He loves me—because He *is* love. His love for me is not based on anything I have ever done or ever could do for Him. It is not based on my performance. I do not deserve His love and could never earn it.

The scripture says that when I was His enemy, *He loved me*. You say, "How could you have been God's enemy when you were a little girl?"

According to the Bible, from the moment I was born, I was ungodly, a sinner, God's enemy, and deserving of His eternal wrath (Romans 5:6–10). In spite of my alienation from Him, He loved me and sent His Son to die for me. He loved me in eternity past; He will love me for all of eternity future. There is nothing I could do to make Him love me any less; there is nothing I could do to make Him love me any more.

NANCY LEIGH DEMOSS
Lies Women Believe and the Truth That Sets Them Free

Walking in God-Confidence

If my people, who are called by my name,
will humble themselves and pray and seek my
face. . .then I will hear from heaven,
and I will forgive their sin
and will heal their land.

2 CHRONICLES 7:14 NIV

Some people consider humility a weakness. Others think humility means never talking about yourself or always putting yourself and your accomplishments down. Christians often confuse humility with low self-esteem, believing we should not think of ourselves as worthy, because Jesus Christ was the only perfect person.

But when we accept Christ as our Lord and Savior, His life becomes ours. We are no longer slaves to sin, but we own His righteousness. So we don't have to go around thinking that we're scum. Since God reconciled us to Himself through Jesus' sacrifice on the cross, we can live each day with the confidence of knowing we're forgiven.

Our Savior walked in total God-confidence—knowing that His steps were planned—and He had only to listen to His Father's heartbeat to know which way to go. He could withstand insults, persecutions, and dim-witted disciples because He knew who He was and where He was headed.

Today, humble yourself in front of God and ask His forgiveness for the ways you've sinned. Accept His forgiveness and live in total God-confidence, knowing that He has heard you. Then you'll be able to withstand the pressures life throws at you, because He is your life.

DENA DYER
Daily Encouragement for Single Women

The Heart's Truth

Jesus asked, "You of little faith, why are you talking among yourselves about having no bread? Do you still not understand? Don't you remember the five loaves for the five thousand, and how many basketfuls you gathered? . . . How is it you don't understand that I was not talking to you about bread?"

MATTHEW 16:8–11 NIV

Until the will and the affections are brought under the authority of Christ, we have not begun to understand, let alone to accept, His lordship. The cross, as it enters the love life, will reveal the heart's truth. My heart, I knew, would be forever a lonely hunter unless settled "where true joys are to be found."

One morning I was reading the story of Jesus' feeding of the five thousand. The disciples could find only five loaves of bread and two fishes. "Let me have them," said Jesus. He asked for all. He took them, said the blessing, and broke them before He gave them out. I remembered what a chapel speaker, Ruth Stull of Peru, has said: "If my life is broken when given to Jesus, it is because pieces will feed a multitude, while a loaf will satisfy only a little lad."

ELISABETH ELLIOT
Passion and Purity

Pressed, Yet Peaceful

Master, the multitude throng thee
and press thee. . . . And he said unto her,
Daughter, be of good comfort:
thy faith hath made thee whole; go in peace.
LUKE 8:45, 48 KJV

Many know that crushed feeling. I think our
Lord must have thought of how often his followers would be "pressed out of measure, above
strength," as one of them said, because of the
throng of things, and because power had gone
out of them; and so He allowed this lovely story
to be told. Thronged, pressed, crushed, tired—
for a man is tired when, in some special way,
power has gone forth from him, and as He was
man as well as God He must have been tired
then—yet He was so peaceful that He could
bring peace to the one who was fearing and
trembling.

The more one ponders such a story, the more one sees in it, and the more one longs to live that life of victory over circumstances, the life which, though outwardly crowded and crushed, is yet overflowing with peace.

May the peace of our dear Lord fill every hour with peace today.

AMY CARMICHAEL
Edges of His Ways

An Exhortation

Then David continued, "Be strong and
courageous, and do the work.
*Don't be afraid or discouraged, for the L*ORD
God, my God, is with you.
He will not fail you or forsake you."
1 CHRONICLES 28:20 NLT

In 1 Chronicles 28:20, King David has just
given his son Solomon and the people of Israel
detailed instructions for building the Lord's
temple. Can you imagine how awed and overwhelmed the people felt as they heard the plans
for the temple's design? First Kings 5 and 6 tell
us that it took *tens of thousands* of skilled work-
men *seven years* to complete the temple! No
wonder David exhorted his people to be strong
and courageous! No wonder he urged them to
resist discouragement and fear!

God knew His people could complete

the undertaking He had set before them, but He also knew they would be overwhelmed by the enormity of the task. Perhaps you, too, are feeling disheartened by the sheer size of your responsibilities. Maybe you feel like giving up. David's words still offer us encouragement in the face of the seemingly insurmountable: Be strong and courageous! Do the work! Don't be afraid or discouraged by the size of the task. The Lord God is with you, and He will not fail you or forsake you!

MANDY NYDEGGER
Whispers of Wisdom for Busy Women

You're Not Too Old

"For I know the plans I have for you,"
says the LORD. *"They are plans for good and not*
for disaster, to give you a future and a hope."
JEREMIAH 29:11 NLT

Do you sometimes feel like the best part of your life is already over? That can be the cause of intense unhappiness and dissatisfaction. In fact, several studies have revealed that the older a person gets, the more likely it is that that person will become depressed. It seems old age and depression go hand in hand.

But they don't have to!

No matter what your age, you are not too old to fulfill the plans God has for your life.

Did you know that Grandma Moses started painting at age seventy-six? Without any art classes or special training, she painted simple, realistic pictures of rural settings—paintings of historic importance.

So what dreams has God placed inside you? Is it to write a book? To start your own business? What's holding you back? In Jeremiah 29:11, God said He had good plans for His people. Don't you think He has a good plan for you?

If you feel like you're too old, ask God to change your perception of yourself. He wants you to realize your dreams because He's the One who put them there.

Jesus came to give you a full life. But you have to want it, too! Spend some time today meditating on your dreams—even those you have let go of—and commit to praying over them until they are realized. That faithfulness in itself will bring happiness and hope.

MICHELLE MEDLOCK ADAMS
Secrets of Happiness

Doing Good Work

For we are his workmanship, created in
Christ Jesus unto good works,
which God hath before ordained that
we should walk in them.
EPHESIANS 2:10 KJV

When we create something, it feels good to know we've done a good job. As we put the final touches on a report, a letter, or whatever widgets we make on the job, gladness fills us, not just that we've finished the job, but that we've done it well.

God enjoys creating things, too—like people. Imagine how He felt when He finished creating you. Did He smile, knowing He'd finished a masterpiece? Could He trust that here was a person who would do good works for Him out of deep love?

We may make a widget and never see it

again. It becomes part of a car, building, or computer. A report or letter gets filed away, and few see it after the fact. But that's not so with God; He sees us every day of our lives and watches us fondly as we do the good works He prepared for us to accomplish. When that work is finished, He calls us home because He made us and wants to share eternity with us.

Is the work you're doing today something that will make the Creator proud?

Lord, thank You for making me to do good things that make You proud. Help me do those things today.

PAMELA L. MCQUADE
Daily Wisdom for the Workplace

When We Need Help

"My sheep listen to my voice; I know them,
and they follow me. I give them eternal life,
and they shall never perish; no one will
snatch them out of my hand."
JOHN 10:27–28 NIV

As a college student I worried much about whether I would fail to follow the Shepherd, would be deaf to His call. I thought it such a bewildering matter.

It is not a worry anymore. Experience has taught me that the Shepherd is far more willing to show His sheep the path than the sheep are to follow. He is endlessly merciful, patient, tender, and loving. If we, His stupid and wayward sheep, really want to be led, we will without fail be led. Of that I am sure.

When we need help, we wish we knew somebody who was wise enough to tell us what to do, reachable when we need him, and even able to help us. God is. Omniscient, omnipresent, omnipotent—everything we need. The issue is confidence in the Shepherd Himself, a confidence so complete that we offer ourselves without any reservation whatsoever and determine to do what He says.

ELISABETH ELLIOT
Keep a Quiet Heart

Worship and Rest

Return to your rest, my soul,
for the LORD has been good to you.
PSALM 116:7 NIV

I can't do it!" I cried to God in prayer shortly after Michael and I were married. "I can't handle the dishes—I can't handle the house—I can't handle my work—I can't handle the loneliness of being the wife of someone who works all the time—I can't deal with my own emotional ups and downs, let alone his! I can't do any of it, God, not any of it!"

I wept before the Lord with a mixture of frustration and guilt over the fact that I was feeling this way about my husband, my home, and my life. God had rescued me from the pit of hell and death just three years before and had given me a hope and a future. How could I— who knew what it was to be hungry and poor and feel there was no love or purpose in life—tell God I couldn't handle these answers to my own prayers?

Fortunately, the Lord did not strike me with lightning; He waited quietly until I was finished and then softly reminded me, *You are trying to do everything in your own strength.* As I sat there in my discouragement, I sensed the Holy Spirit speaking to my heart, saying simply, *All you have to do is worship Me in the midst of what you are facing and I will do the rest.*

"Oh, thank You, Lord," I prayed through my tears. "I think I can at least handle doing that much."

STORMIE OMARTIAN
Finding Peace for Your Heart

Omnipresent God

If I rise on the wings of the dawn,
if I settle on the far side of the sea,
even there your hand will guide me,
your right hand will hold me fast.
PSALM 139:9–10 NIV

Have you ever moved when it wasn't your choice? Maybe it was a job transfer. Or maybe finances required you to downsize from a house to an apartment. It may have been an adjustment to move out on your own after living with roommates. Perhaps you were needed back in your hometown to care for a sick relative. No matter the reason, a move is always somewhat unsettling.

Do you remember as a child when your family went to your grandparents' home for Christmas? Maybe you panicked at the thought of spending the night away from home on

Christmas Eve. What if Santa didn't know where you were?

Think of how unsettling it was to lose a tooth while on vacation. Did the tooth fairy make visits to hotels? How would she ever locate the correct room number in order to deposit the dollar for the tooth under your pillow? Yet Santa and the tooth fairy always showed up! Amazingly, they knew right where you were.

So does God! He is omnipresent, *always present everywhere*. Our human minds cannot conceive it, but it is true. Wherever you live or travel, whatever unfamiliar place you find yourself in, remember God is there with you to guide you and to hold you tight.

EMILY BIGGERS
Daily Encouragement for Single Women

Love Is a Decision

"And now, Israel, what does the LORD your God require of you? He requires only that you fear the LORD your God, and live in a way that pleases him, and love him and serve him with all your heart and soul."

DEUTERONOMY 10:12 NLT

Wouldn't it be great if we could require someone to love us? "But," I can hear you say, "how can you require love? Love is a feeling—you can't require someone to have a certain feeling!"

If love were a feeling, I would agree. But feelings are only a part of love—and a very unreliable part at that.

The love God requires from us for Himself and for each other is the highest form of love—*agape* love—love like His. It is a love of the head rather than a love of the heart. A love that determines to be concerned, first and foremost, for the loved ones' well-being in every dimension of their lives—whatever the cost to ourselves and irrespective of their reaction.

So how can we know that we love God? By being obedient. Jesus said, "Those who accept my commandments and obey them are the ones who love me" (John 14:21 NLT). This verse relieves my anxiety, as I've always worried that I wasn't loving God enough. My fears were based on my erratic feelings toward Him. These words of the Lord take the whole thing out of the realm of feelings and into the realm of doing. Now *that* I can handle! And what can I *do* to show God I love him? I can *do* for others. This is what He requires.

JILL BRISCOE
The One Year Book of Devotions for Women

Speak, Lord

Then call thou, and I will answer.
JOB 13:22 KJV

What about the last time we knelt in prayer? Surely He had more to say to us than we had to say to Him, and yet we never waited a moment to see! We did not give Him opportunity for His gracious response. We rushed away from our King's presence as soon as we had said our say, and vaguely expected Him to send His answers after us somehow and sometime, but not there and then. What wonder if they have not yet reached us! The only wonder is that He ever speaks at all when we act thus. If Mary had talked to the Lord Jesus all the time she sat at His feet, she would not have "heard His word." But is not this pretty much what we have done?

Not that we should pray less, but listen more. And the more we listen, the more we shall want to say afterwards. But we may miss the sweetest whispers of His love by not saying, "Speak, Lord," and not hushing ourselves to "hear what God the Lord will speak." We cannot hear His still, small voice during a torrent of noisy and impatient and hurried petition.

FRANCES RIDLEY HAVERGAL
Daily Thoughts for the King's Children

Encourage and Strengthen Yourself

David was greatly distressed, for the men
spoke of stoning him because the souls
of them all were bitterly grieved, each man for
his sons and daughters.
But David encouraged and strengthened
himself in the Lord his God.
1 SAMUEL 30:6 AMP

We all need people in our lives who encourage and strengthen us. But what about those times when even our most trusted friends are nowhere to be found? Has that ever happened to you? It happened to David. At one of the lowest moments of his life, when his wife and children had been kidnapped, no human being could comfort him because they all had "their own stuff" to deal with.

Fortunately, David had learned something all of us must learn: how to encourage and strengthen himself. We also need to take proactive steps to strengthen ourselves. You can't always rely on someone else. As motivational speaker Jim Rohn put it, "You can't hire someone else to do your push-ups for you."

One thing I do to encourage and strengthen myself is constantly listen to good Bible teaching—in my car, in my bathroom as I get dressed in the morning, in my kitchen while I'm preparing meals or cleaning up. . . . Of course listening to great Bible teachers is not a substitute for spending time in the Word of God.

Affirmation: I encourage and strengthen myself in the Lord.

DONNA PARTOW
Becoming the Woman God Wants Me to Be

Available 24-7

I call on you, my God,
for you will answer me;
turn your ear to me and hear my prayer.
PSALM 17:6 NIV

No one is available to take your call at this time, so leave a message and we will return your call—or not—if we feel like it. . .and only between the hours of 4:00 and 4:30 p.m. Thank you for calling. Have a super day!

We've all felt the frustration of that black hole called voice mail. It is rare to reach a real, honest-to-goodness, breathing human being the first time we dial a telephone number.

Fortunately, our God is always available. He can be reached at any hour of the day or night and every day of the year—including weekends and holidays! When we pray, we don't have to worry about disconnections, hang-ups, or poor reception. We will never be put on hold or our prayers diverted to another department. The Bible assures us that God is eager to hear our petitions and that He welcomes our prayers of thanksgiving. The psalmist David wrote of God's response to those who put their trust in Him: "He will call on me, and I will answer him" (Psalm 91:15 NIV). David had great confidence that God would hear his prayers. And we can, too!

AUSTINE KELLER
Whispers of Wisdom for Busy Women

He Loves Me!

*Behold, what manner of love the Father
hath bestowed upon us, that we should
be called the sons of God.*
1 JOHN 3:1 KJV

"Poor child!" he said in a low voice, as if to himself. "Poor, heartsick, tired child that cannot see what I can see, that its Father's loving arms are all about it!"

I stopped crying, to strain my ears to listen. He went on.

"Katy, all that you say may be true. I daresay it is. But God loves you. He loves you."

"He loves me," I repeated to myself. "He loves me. Oh, Dr. Cabot, if I could believe that! If I could believe that, after all the promises I have broken, all the foolish, wrong things I have done, and shall always be doing, God perhaps still loves me!"

"You may be sure of it," he said solemnly. "I, His minister, bring the gospel to you today. Go home and say over and over to yourself, 'I am a wayward, foolish child. But He loves me! I have disobeyed and grieved Him ten thousand times. But He loves me! I have lost faith in some of my dearest friends and am very desolate. But He loves me! I do not love Him; I am even angry with Him. But He loves me!'"

ELIZABETH PRENTISS
Stepping Heavenward

Giver of Good Things

For the LORD God is a sun and shield;
the LORD will give grace and glory;
no good thing will He withhold from
those who walk uprightly.
PSALM 84:11 NKJV

Worry is such a useless practice, like spinning wheels on a vehicle that takes you nowhere. And yet we women are notorious for it. The Bible advises us to let each day take care of itself. We are promised that God will provide for us.

Psalm 84:11 says that God is not a withholder of good things from His children. He knows us. He created us and put in us our own unique dreams, preferences, and hopes. When you begin to worry, read this verse. Put it on your bulletin board at work and your bathroom mirror at home. Read it aloud each time that worry begins to creep in.

Your heavenly Father is not "the big man upstairs" looking down upon you and laughing at the unfulfilled desires in your life. He wants to give you good things. Often His timing is different than ours, but His plan is always to bless and never to harm us. Look for the blessings in each day, and keep bringing your desires before the Lord in expectation.

EMILY BIGGERS
Daily Encouragements for Single Women

A Place in the World

*The Spirit of God has made me; the breath of
the Almighty gives me life.*
JOB 33:4 NIV

A poor little blind girl, without influential
friends, could have as many ambitions as anyone; but how was she to achieve them? What
was there for her? The great world that could
see was rushing past me day by day, and sweep-
ing on toward the goal of its necessities and
desires; while I was left stranded by the way-
side. "Oh, you cannot do this—because you
are blind, you know; you can never go there,
because it would not be worthwhile: you could
not see anything if you did, you know"—these
and other things were often said to me, in reply
to my many and eager questionings.

Often, when such circumstances as this made me very blue and depressed, I would creep off alone, kneel down, and ask God if, though blind, I was not one of His children—if in all His great world He had not some little place for me. And it often seemed that I could hear Him say, "Do not be discouraged, little girl; you shall someday be happy and useful, even in your blindness." And I would go back among my associates, cheered and encouraged and feeling that it would not be very long before my life would be full of activity and usefulness.

FANNY CROSBY
Memories of Eighty Years

He Wants to Hold Your Hand

> "I will lead the blind by ways they have
> not known, along unfamiliar paths I will
> guide them; I will turn the darkness into
> light before them and make the rough places
> smooth. These are the things I will do;
> I will not forsake them."
>
> Isaiah 42:16 NIV

About fifteen years ago I called my mom while gulping back sobs and told her I felt like my life was falling apart. I was in the middle of a difficult job change, a good friend had been killed in a car accident, and I'd just found out that another friend was having an affair. I was disillusioned and depressed and said I could no longer see the proverbial light at the end of the tunnel.

Mom listened to me for a long time and then told me that I should start reading the book of Isaiah. She said he had a lot to say about dark, desperate places. I must admit I wasn't initially enthused or encouraged by her advice. I didn't want her to tell me to study some ancient prophet—I wanted her to FedEx a plane ticket to a tropical island!

But when I finally shut down my pity party and perused Isaiah, I discovered that mushrooms aren't the only things that grow in the dark. So does faith.

Reading this Old Testament prophecy didn't make the clouds in my life immediately vanish. It simply reminded me to pause and pray, to be still and listen for divine directions, and to quit whining and let God lead me.

LISA HARPER
What the Bible Is All About for Women

Mirror, Mirror

I praise you because of the wonderful way you created me. Everything you do is marvelous!
PSALM 139:14 CEV

How do you see yourself? Do you have a negative perception? When you look in the mirror, do you see a child of the Most High King, or do you focus on your flaws? If you're like most people, you probably see the imperfections.

Women, especially, struggle with self-esteem.

Ask God to help you see yourself as He sees you. God thinks you're amazing. He doesn't mind if your thighs aren't model thin or your hair is a bit on the frizzy side. He thinks you're wonderful, and He wants you to think you're wonderful, too.

Remember that old saying, "God doesn't make any junk"? Well, it's as true today as when we learned it in vacation Bible school. You are priceless. You are far more precious than rubies. You have got it going on in God's eyes. After all, He created you!

Let God's love shine big in you, and forget about those size 6 jeans that no longer fit. Sure, it's okay to work on your outer appearance, but don't let that consume you. Let God's love overwhelm you and spill out onto all the people around you. Get up every day, look in the mirror, and say, "I may not be perfect, but I am perfectly loved." Starting each day with that confession will put you on the road to happiness—even if you're having a bad hair day. Just grab a cute hat and greet the world with love and happiness in your heart.

MICHELLE MEDLOCK ADAMS
Secrets of Happiness

My Savior, My Bridegroom

This is how God showed his love among us:
He sent his one and only Son into the world
that we might live through him. This is love:
not that we loved God, but that he loved us
and sent his Son as an atoning
sacrifice for our sins.
1 JOHN 4:9–10 NIV

Christ also hath loved us, and given Himself
for us." "The Son of God. . .loved me, and gave
Himself for me." Yes, Himself! What is the
Bride's true and central treasure? What calls
forth the deepest, brightest, sweetest thrill of
love and praise? Not the Bridegroom's priceless
gifts, not the robe of His resplendent righteousness, not the dowry of unsearchable riches, not
the magnificence of the palace home to which
He is bringing her, not the glory which she shall
share with Him, but Himself! Jesus Christ,

"who His own self bare our sins in His own body on the tree"; "this same Jesus," "whom having not seen, ye love"; the Son of God and the Man of Sorrows; my Savior, my Friend, my Master, my King, my Priest, my Lord, and my God—He says, "*I* also for thee!" What an "*I*"! What power and sweetness we feel in it, so different from any human "I," for all His Godhead and all His manhood are concentrated in it, and all "for thee"!

Frances Ridley Havergal
Kept for the Master's Use

The Comfort of God

*I will pray the Father, and he shall give you
another Comforter, that he may abide with
you for ever; even the Spirit of truth;
whom the world cannot receive, because
it seeth him not, neither knoweth him:
but ye know him; for he dwelleth with
you, and shall be in you.*
JOHN 14:16–17 KJV

Two little girls were talking about God, and
one said, "I know God does not love me. He could
not care for such a teeny, tiny little girl as I am."

"Dear me, sis," said the other little girl,
"don't you know that that is just what God is
for—to take care of teeny, tiny little girls who
can't take care of themselves, just like us?"

"Is He?" said the first little girl. "I did not
know that. Then I don't need to worry anymore,
do I?"

If any troubled doubting heart, any heart that is fearing continually every day some form or other of evil should read these lines, let me tell you again in trumpet tones that this is just what the Lord Jesus Christ is for—to care for and comfort all who mourn.

"All," remember, every single one, even you yourself, for it would not be "all" if you were left out. You may be so cast down that you can hardly lift up your head, but the apostle tells us that He is the "God that comforteth those that are cast down;" the comforting of Christ. All who mourn, all who are cast down—I love to think of such a mission of comfort in a world of mourning like ours; and I long to see every cast down and sorrowing heart comforted with this comforting of God.

HANNAH WHITALL SMITH
The God of All Comfort

Holding Out for a Hero

*Think about Jesus, who was sent to us and is
the high priest of our faith. Jesus was faithful
to God as Moses was in God's family. . . .
But Christ is faithful as a Son over God's
house. And we are God's house if we
confidently maintain our hope.*
HEBREWS 3:1–2, 6 NCV

Every now and then when I can't see around
the corner of my circumstances or when I feel
alone or misunderstood, I whine for a different kind of Messiah. One who will make all
my messes disappear. One who will answer my
prayer for a husband and children. One who
will make my closest friends interested listeners, conscientious encouragers, and fatter than
me. Sometimes I just wish our Hero of a Savior
would make my life less hard.

Of course, a Savior like that only exists in

fairy tales and isn't really very heroic. A Messiah who only serves to grant our wishes would be akin to an overly indulgent mother who lets her child eat all the candy he wants, stay up as late as he likes, and never makes him accept responsibility or obey authority. Pretty soon she's got a middle-aged man with no job, no friends, and no respect for her still living in his boyhood room and demanding Twinkies for lunch. And if we had a Messiah like that, we'd be no better off.

LISA HARPER
Holding Out for a Hero

Content in Him

But godliness with contentment is great gain.
1 TIMOTHY 6:6 KJV

Even the strongest Christian can struggle with discontentment. We're conditioned by the world to want more—of everything. More money, nicer clothes, a bigger house, a better-paying job. We're rarely satisfied with what we have.

And when we're single, the "I Wish I Had This or That" list can get pretty long. If we don't get the things we long for—a spouse, children, a home, a better car, or nicer clothes—sometimes our discontentment shifts into overdrive. But what can we do about it?

Today, take stock of what God has already done for you. Take a look at the areas of your life in which you've been struggling with discontentment. Hasn't God already given you people who pour into your life? Hasn't He made sure you have a roof over your head and food to eat? Has He not provided you a way to get to and from work?

Instead of focusing on all of the things you don't have, spend some time praising Him for the things you do have. Offer the Lord any discontentment, and watch Him give you a contented heart.

JANICE HANNA
Daily Encouragement for Single Women

Safe in His Arms

He tends his flock like a shepherd:
He gathers the lambs in his arms
and carries them close to his heart.

Isaiah 40:11 NIV

As a chaplain, I hear many inspiring stories from the elderly persons I serve. However, there are some days that are emotionally heavy due to their pain and struggles.

On one particularly "heavy" day, I walked into the room of a woman who was once a vibrant Christian woman. She is no longer able to feed herself, walk, or talk. As I prayed over her, I asked the Lord, "Why so much injustice, so much pain?" My eyes left her and moved to a picture hanging above her bed—a picture I had never noticed before. Jesus stood in the center surrounded by sheep. In one hand he held a staff and in the other, a lamb. The lamb was resting

securely in its Shepherd's arms, cradled against His chest. At that moment, I knew the answer to my question. It's as if God was saying, "I never intended for the pain and the injustice. This world is broken, but I am here *through* the pain. I will carry her through this." It was clear—she was the lamb He held in His arms. We are the sheep that follow Him, and when one of us is in need, our Father and Shepherd picks us up and holds us close.

Today, let's be reminded that even though trials and tears may come, we are not alone. Jesus carries the helpless and dependent. He carries you and me.

JOCELYN HAMSHER
Circle of Friends

The Power of Encouragement

"But my mouth would encourage you;
comfort from my lips would bring you relief."
JOB 16:5 NIV

The truest earthly friends are those who share their faith in our heavenly Father. The best biblical example of friendship is that of David and Jonathan. Even though his father, King Saul, seemed determined to kill David, Jonathan told his friend, "Whatsoever thy soul desireth, I will even do it for thee" (1 Samuel 20:4 KJV). Not only did Jonathan clothe David with friendship, but he armed him as well.

In 1 Samuel, Jonathan made covenants with David as well as informed him of danger, helped to rescue him, prayed for him, appealed to God for him, and bound him to himself with promises. At their last encounter, "Jonathan. . . went to David into the wood, and strengthened his hand in God. And he said unto him, Fear not: for the hand of Saul my father shall not find thee; and thou shalt be king over Israel, and I shall be next unto thee; and that also Saul my father knoweth. And they two made a covenant before the LORD: and David abode in the wood, and Jonathan went to his house" (1 Samuel 23:16–18 KJV). What a friendship!

Each and every day, make it a point to encourage your friends through prayer, comfort, service, listening, and blessings. But most of all, love them, as Jonathan loved David, as Jesus loves us.

Tap into the power of encouragement and love from the greatest resource at our disposal, our greatest Friend—our one and only Savior, Jesus Christ. He will never leave us nor forsake us.

DONNA K. MALTESE
Power Prayers to Start Your Day

Honorable Living

But God chose the foolish things of the world to shame the wise; God chose the weak things of the world to shame the strong.

1 Corinthians 1:27 niv

Maybe you aren't in management, or if you are, you may feel as if you're still on a very low rung of the ladder. If you work for people who have a lot of smarts, it's easy to start feeling as if you have nothing of value to offer. After all, aren't these other folks so much better than you?

Be encouraged. God isn't just looking for the really smart, the really gifted, or the really wealthy to do His work. In fact, He seems to prefer to use the quiet, lowly, but perfectly obedient person.

You may not reach a high position in your job. Perhaps you'll stay pretty much where you are now for as long as you stay with this company. But whatever your place, if your life honors God, your faith can have a powerful impact on your workplace.

You might not get a promotion because someone thinks you're "too honest." You might watch others pass you by because they played some office-politics games you stepped back from. But people will remember you and recognize the things you stood for. A few may even feel shame and wish they'd followed in your footsteps.

Lord, no matter where You want to use me, I want to be Your servant. Let my light shine for You today.

PAMELA L. McQUADE
Daily Wisdom for the Workplace

God in the Driver's Seat

*I will instruct thee and teach thee in
the way which thou shalt go:
I will guide thee with mine eye.*
PSALM 32:8 KJV

Hannah came to a fork in the road. She had to make some life-changing decisions. The hardest part was that the decisions she made would significantly affect the lives of her loved ones. What was she to do?

God tells us that whenever we have a decision to make, He will instruct and teach us. He will not let us flounder; but as we seek His face, He will provide direction, understanding, wisdom, and insight. He will teach us the way—the road, the path, or the journey we need to take that is in our best interest. We can clearly comprehend the way we should walk because God is guiding, with His eye upon us. He is

omniscient, which means He knows all things. He knows our past, our present, and our future. He sees and understands what we are not able to comprehend in our finite beings. What a blessing that an all-knowing Lord will guide us!

TINA C. ELACQUA
Whispers of Wisdom for Busy Women

Created by God

So God created mankind in his own image,
in the image of God he created them;
male and female he created them.

GENESIS 1:27 NIV

A whole new year stretches out before you, like a crisp carpet of newly fallen snow. What kind of footprints will you leave? Maybe your strides will be gigantic leaps of faith. Or perhaps you will take tiny steps of slow, steady progress. Some imprints might even be creative expressions, woman-sized angels in the snow.

You are a woman; you were created in God's own image. But that isn't the message our world peddles. So what does it mean to be created in God's image? For starters, you have imagination, intellect, and most importantly, a soul. That's the deepest part of your being, where you long to feel whole, loved, cherished, and understood.

But hold the phone: God made you so that He might have an ongoing relationship with you. You need Him and He's promised to always be there for you. Isn't that the kind of life companion you've searched for?

On her fifty-fifth birthday a close friend confided in me that she's never felt really loved by anyone. "That's not true," I told her. "God loves you." Hopefully during this year she'll understand that God has been there all along. She just didn't take time to look in His Word. She didn't take time to feel His love.

CAROL L. FITZPATRICK
Daily Wisdom for Women

Financial Strain

*"No one can serve two masters.
Either you will hate the one and love
the other, or you will be devoted to the
one and despise the other. You cannot
serve both God and money."*

MATTHEW 6:24 NIV

Do you ever get nervous when you watch the
news and see reports about the stock market?
Does your head spin when you see the prices
rise at the gas pump? Can you feel your heart
race when you look at your bills in comparison
to your bank statement? Even though many of
our day-to-day activities depend on money, it's
important to remember that money is not a
provider or sustainer. Only God can provide for
you and sustain you. When we begin to focus
on and worry about money, then we are telling
God that we don't trust Him.

As you feel yourself start to worry about money, stop and change your focus from wealth to God. Thank Him for what He has provided for you and then humbly ask Him to give you wisdom about your financial situation. Be at peace as you remember that you can absolutely trust God to provide for you and to sustain you.

SARAH MAE RATLIFF
Daily Encouragement for Single Women

Singing the Blue
Jeans Blues

*Not that I have already obtained all this,
or have already arrived at my goal,
but I press on to take hold of that for
which Christ Jesus took hold of me.*

PHILIPPIANS 3:12 NIV

We've all been there. You go to the mall with high hopes and high self-esteem, ready to buy a new pair of jeans. Seventy-two pairs later, your legs are raw from trying them on and your self-esteem is lower than a snake's belly.

Jeans are a part of every gal's wardrobe, but finding a pair that fits every curve and hides every bulge can be challenging.

Still, we press on—determined to find the jeans that won't make our hind ends look flat and wide. Sometimes this quest may take days, even weeks. But, eventually, we will succeed. We're women—shopping challenges don't faze us.

If only we were that steadfast when it comes to other areas of our lives—especially spiritual battles. Have you found yourself throwing in the faith towel before you see your victory come to pass?

It's easy to do. Evangelist Chip Brim once shared that God had shown him a vision of Christians on a football field. They were collapsing on the one-yard line. They were so close to their breakthroughs, but they simply grew weary and quit inches from their victory.

Chip said it made him very sad to see so many Christians quitting before they'd realized their breakthroughs. The Bible says you can do all things through Christ Jesus. Don't quit just short of your victory. The reward is even better than finding that perfect pair of blue jeans.

MICHELLE MEDLOCK ADAMS
Secrets of Beauty

Vocalizing a Prayer

And when you are praying, do not use
meaningless repetition as the Gentiles do,
for they suppose that they will be heard
for their many words.

MATTHEW 6:7 NASB

Remember kneeling beside your bed and praying when you were a kid? Why did it all seem so simple then? We just talked to God like He was really there and kept our requests short and simple.

Then, as you got older, the lengthy and spiritual prayers of the "older saints" became intimidating. So where's the balance? Reading a little further in this passage from Matthew, at verse 9, Jesus gives us His own example for prayer. If you can remember the acrostic ACTS, you'll have an excellent formula for prayer: Adoration, Confession, Thanksgiving, and Supplication.

As we come before the Lord, we first need to honor Him as Creator, Master, Savior, and Lord. Reflect on who He is and praise Him. And because we're human, we need to confess and repent of our daily sins. Following this we should be in a mode of thanksgiving. Finally, our prayer requests should be upheld. My usual order for requests is self, family members, and life's pressing issues. Keeping a prayer journal allows for a written record of God's answers.

Your prayers certainly don't have to be elaborate or polished. God does not judge your way with words. He knows your heart. He wants to hear from you.

CAROL L. FITZPATRICK
Daily Wisdom for Women

Focusing on Pleasing God

Am I now trying to win the approval of human beings, or of God? Or am I trying to please people? If I were still trying to please people, I would not be a servant of Christ.
GALATIANS 1:10 NIV

We all have those days when it seems we are disappointing everyone around us. Your coworker expected you to drop your projects and help her with hers, but you had hoped she would be able to do the same for you. Your best friend let you borrow her favorite handmade scarf for a date, and you accidentally spilled your café mocha on it. Your sister called to ask if you'd watch your niece while she takes your nephew to a doctor's appointment, but you've already made plans for the afternoon. There are even days when we feel that we have been doing almost more than we can do and still we have people displeased and angry with us.

Praise God that He sees us as valuable, even though we don't always do things perfectly. Thank God that He doesn't expect us to say yes to every request that we receive. Focus your time on listening to how God wants you to serve Him and the people in your life, but don't be discouraged when you discover you can't please everyone.

SARAH MAE RATLIFF
Daily Encouragement for Single Women

Caring for the Temple

Honor God with your body.
1 Corinthians 6:20 NLT

Our bodies are an amazing gift from God. Without any thought or effort on our parts, our hearts beat life-giving blood throughout our veins, providing us with the energy to accomplish the thousands of tasks we do each day. Our brains give the commands; our bodies obey. But these incredible structures aren't maintenance free. Just as we are to be good stewards of our resources of time and money, we should also be good stewards of our bodies. God's Word calls them a temple.

When we are busy meeting the needs of others, we often neglect to care for ourselves. But God wants us to treat our bodies with care and respect. This means exercising regularly, eating good food, getting enough rest. These

are simple things, but the dividends are high, for when we treat our bodies right, they treat us right in return.

JOANNA BLOSS
To Love and to Cherish

Repent and Be Restored

And I will restore to you the years that
the locust hath eaten, the cankerworm,
and the caterpillar, and the palmerworm,
my great army which I sent among you.
JOEL 2:25 KJV

Throughout scripture we encounter a divine
paradox, an apparent contradiction in the way
God intervenes in human history: the God who
chastens His people is the same God who turns
around and blesses them.

We see this over and over in the history
of Israel. God directs Israel; Israel follows for
a while but then turns away and commits sin.
God chastises His people, destroying their crops
or sending them into exile. When they repent,
He has pity on them and blesses them again.

The key is repentance.

Our hearts must turn from ourselves to our

Lord. God is so gracious, forgiving, and loving that a mustard seed of repentance grows a whole tree of blessing. God restores what was lost, even when He knows there will be future failures.

Have the locusts been eating away at your marriage? Have there been mistakes and failures? Has your pride caused contentions in your house? If so, repent. Turn from your foolish ways and obey Him.

He will cause His face to shine upon you. And will restore the years the locusts ate.

HELEN WIDGER MIDDLEBROOKE
To Love and to Cherish

Words of Wisdom from Eleanor Roosevelt

As God's chosen people, holy and dearly loved,
clothe yourselves with compassion, kindness,
humility, gentleness and patience.
COLOSSIANS 3:12 NIV

Eleanor Roosevelt has been called the most revered woman of her generation. She not only gave birth to six children, but also served as a dynamic political helpmate to her husband, Franklin Delano Roosevelt.

Eleanor Roosevelt literally transformed the role of First Lady, holding press conferences, traveling to all parts of the country, giving lectures and radio broadcasts, and expressing her opinions in a daily syndicated newspaper column called "My Day." You might say that she was a woman on a mission, a servant to human-kind, and a role model for all women.

Knowing of her accomplishments, it was very interesting to discover Mrs. Roosevelt was a very shy and awkward child. It wasn't until she began attending a distinguished school in England that she began to develop self-confidence. During that self-discovery phase, she wrote, "No matter how plain a woman may be, if truth and loyalty are stamped upon her face, all will be attracted to her."

What wise words from such a young teen, huh? If only we all understood that truth.

If you're feeling plain, unworthy, unattract-ive, and unnoticed—give yourself a makeover from the inside out. Ask God to develop the fruits of the Spirit within you, and allow the Lord to fill you with His love. Pretty soon, you'll be confident and irresistible. And you'll make a difference every place you go!

MICHELLE MEDLOCK ADAMS
Secrets of Beauty

Put On the New

And provide for those who grieve in Zion—
to bestow on them a crown of beauty instead
of ashes, the oil of joy instead of mourning,
and a garment of praise instead
of a spirit of despair. They will be called oaks
of righteousness, a planting of the LORD
for the display of his splendor.
ISAIAH 61:3 NIV

I have to admit I'm a sucker for those fashion makeover shows. I love the one where the guy and girl ambush some poor unsuspecting person and help them buy a brand-new wardrobe. But the catch is that the victim has to be willing to throw away all of their old clothes.

I'm amazed that anyone would put up a fight—but they almost always do! I mean, what on earth could be hanging in someone's closet that they wouldn't gladly toss out to replace it with something new? And yet I have seen people pleading to keep their worn-out bunny slippers and tie-dyed T-shirts.

When you think about it, aren't we just as crazy? Our Father God has—through Christ— given us the opportunity to shed a spirit of heaviness and replace it with a garment of praise. But we sometimes have trouble letting go of the heaviness.

And that's when He comes to the rescue again, taking us by the hand, guiding us, and gently helping us cast off the old and put on the new.

SUZIE THOMAS
Circle of Friends

What's Holding You Back?

Thank you for making me so wonderfully complex! Your workmanship is marvelous—how well I know it.

PSALM 139:14 NLT

Fanny Crosby, the author of more than nine thousand hymns and another one thousand secular poems and songs, never let her physical challenges stop the call she felt on her life. And she never let her disability become a hindrance in her relationship with God.

Born in 1820, Fanny had her vision at birth. But at six weeks, she suffered an eye inflammation. The family's usual doctor wasn't available, so they sought help from a man who claimed to be medically qualified to help. He put a poultice on Fanny's eyes, leaving the infant's eyes scarred. The "doctor" left town—and Fanny blind.

Growing up blind wasn't easy, but Fanny didn't blame God for her situation. She didn't ask, "Why me?" Instead, she determined in her heart to make a difference in this world.

When adversity happens in life, people respond in different ways. Some get angry with God. And some become even more determined to reach their goals and dreams—like Fanny.

If you've been dealing with a painful disability or if you've been emotionally crippled due to circumstances beyond your control, God cares. Despite your troubles, God's plan for you has never changed, and His plan is a good one!

If you don't know the plan that God has for you, ask Him to show you. Tell Him that you are ready to carry out all that He has for you to do. Like Fanny, you are an important part of His overall plan in this world.

MICHELLE MEDLOCK ADAMS
Secrets of Beauty

Receiving God's Embrace

*See what great love the Father has lavished on
us, that we should be called children of God!
And that is what we are!*
1 JOHN 3:1 NIV

Some people are born "huggers." They greet
family members or complete strangers in the
same way—with a hug. They just can't help
themselves. They must lavish love on those
around them. They must demonstrate affection. Most of us would agree that the closer the
relationship, the more meaningful the hug. Can
you imagine receiving an embrace from our
heavenly Father, the God of the universe?

God lavished His love on us when He sent
Jesus to earth. Jesus' sacrificial death on our be-
half paved the way for adoption into God's family by faith. When we receive the gift of Jesus,
we become children of God. We are no longer

strangers. We are no longer alienated from a holy God. We have become family!

As you ponder God's great love for you, picture Jesus hanging on the cross. With arms outstretched, He not only came to embrace the world with God's love; He came to embrace you! Will you receive God's hug? The unconditional love of our Creator is the greatest gift we could ever receive. Will you allow His love to be lavished upon you? Receive the embrace of your heavenly Father today!

JULIE RAYBURN
To Love and to Cherish

Confidence to Go Beyond

"Have I not commanded you?
Be strong and of good courage; do not be
afraid, nor be dismayed, for the LORD your
God is with you wherever you go."
JOSHUA 1:9 NKJV

Sometimes confidence is found in the most unlikely of places. For writer, speaker, and interior designer Ann Platz, this place was the pantry of her new home.

The author of thirteen books, Ann speaks regularly to a variety of groups and has even written about the courage of women who have shown great faith in the face of adversity.

Past successes, however, don't always mean having confidence in future endeavors. Women who seek to grow and expand, in both their faith and their personal goals, often find themselves facing tasks that far exceed their current abilities. Or so they may believe.

Ann found an answer to those doubts when she moved into her new home. Ann writes, "I discovered this scripture, Joshua 1:9, printed on a business-sized card, in the pantry of my new home. The house had belonged to the estate of a woman I greatly admired, Mrs. Grace Kinser. Later I realized that this message 'left behind' would be a life message to me. I framed the card. Many a day I have been challenged beyond my abilities and have sought great spiritual strength and confidence from this printed message of grace from Grace."

When we believe our own abilities will fail us, we can turn our minds and hearts outward, relying on the One who never fails. God, who is always with us, will give us the strength and courage to face—and conquer—whatever challenges lie before us.

RAMONA RICHARDS
Secrets of Confidence

The Power of Creative Vision

Be careful how you live. Don't live like fools,
but like those who are wise.
Make the most of every opportunity.
EPHESIANS 5:15–16 NLT

Many people look back upon their lives as a series of missed opportunities. Are you one of them?

Take the following steps to ensure that you make the most of every opportunity in the future:

First, *pray for creative vision*. Take your ideas to Jesus, the One by whom "all things were created... visible and invisible" (Colossians 1:16 NKJV). Jesus is just waiting for you to prayerfully present your dreams and ideas to Him.

Second, *listen expectantly*. After you have prayed for creative vision, be still, open your mind, and *expect* God to speak to you. God shares your dreams *with* you.

Third, begin to *pay attention* to what is around you. Keep your eyes open to the "creative possibilities" surrounding you!

Fourth, be *resourceful*. Sometimes, when God is calling us into a certain area, we need to *make* our own opportunities.

And last, *have courage*. Sometimes it seems easier to stay anchored in the place where we feel the most comfortable. But that place may not be where God wants us to be. Courage is needed to set sail into unknown waters.

Pray for creative vision, expect God to speak to you, pay attention to the winds blowing around you, be resourceful, and then courageously set sail, confident that God has given you the ability to take advantage of every opportunity He affords you. Remember that you are never alone: God will be with you throughout your voyage, steering you through every ocean!

DONNA K. MALTESE
Power Prayers to Start Your Day

Giving Our Best

Honor the LORD with your wealth,
with the firstfruits of all your crops;
then your barns will be filled to overflowing,
and your vats will brim over with new wine.
PROVERBS 3:9–10 NIV

When God talks about pure offerings, He's dead serious. And when He says to give Him the firstfruits of our produce, He's referring to the very best, not inexpensive substitutes.

Of course, not as many people make a living in agriculture anymore. We don't all pay our bills by farming or put jars of olives in the collection plate on Sunday. And the closest most of us come to sheep is wearing wool in the winter. So I've written "heart and mind" next to Proverbs 3:9–10 in my Bible. Because I think the context of *firstfruits* can be expanded to include our time and attention.

In other words, we should be thinking about God more than anyone else. He should be more important to us than anything. Instead of slinking toward Him with scratch-and-dent sacrifices, we should run to Him with offerings we've spent our whole allowance on. And we should be able to stand before Him with big silly grins—like kindergarteners with a plaster-of-paris handprint we made all by ourselves— knowing that He's going to love what we've brought Him!

LISA HARPER
Tough Love, Tender Mercies

You Are Wanted

So God created mankind in his own image,
in the image of God he created them;
male and female he created them.
GENESIS 1:27 NIV

Are you a creative person? Do you like to arrange photos in artful ways to make a scrapbook? Maybe you enjoy fashioning beads and metals into a beautiful piece of jewelry. Perhaps arranging flowers in a vase gives you a sense of joy and satisfaction.

Think for a moment about what started your endeavor. At the very basic level, you wanted whatever it was that you set out to create. One woman paints because she wants a picture. Another knits because she wants a scarf.

Have you ever thought about why God created us? Genesis records how God formed the earth, sea, and sky. He filled them with fish and birds, plants and animals. And when everything was ready for human habitation, he created man and woman.

God wanted us. That has been His desire from the beginning. When sin separated us from God, He made a way back by sending His Son to die for us. The precious blood of Christ holds the power of redemption and reconciliation.

Jesus prayed in John 17:24 (NIV), "Father, I want those you have given me to be with me where I am, and to see my glory." Jesus wants to be with us! If we have given our hearts to Him, we belong to Him.

> *If you're here, then you were made.*
> *If you were made, then you are loved.*
> *If you are loved. . .*
> *There's a reason that you're here.*

You are wanted!

JULIE HUFSTETLER
Singer, Songwriter

Let Your Joy Shine!

*But let all those that put their trust in thee
rejoice: let them ever shout for joy,
because thou defendest them: let them also
that love thy name be joyful in thee.*
PSALM 5:11 KJV

If there is anything that is missing from the
Christian home these days, it's a smile.

Weighed down by unreasonable expecta-
tions, impossible schedules, and just the daily
grind of life, we become stressed and sullen.
Smiles disappear at the first hint of tension.

Why do we open our homes to the thiev-
ing pressures that rob us of joy? Why do we so
easily forget the great things that God has done
and is doing for us?

God is our redeemer. Our defender. Our
rock. Our high tower. Our hope. Our deliverer.
Our shield. Our strength. Our salvation.

We are forgiven. Justified. Sanctified. Made holy.

Our bodies are the temple of the Holy Spirit. He is *in* us, and we are in Him. Nothing—death, life, angels, principalities, powers, the future, the past, things in the heavens or the deep, or any other creature (even our faithless selves)—absolutely *nothing* can separate us from the love of God in Christ Jesus our Lord.

If we would truly grasp just *one* of these truths, our lives and our faces would be light and cheerful.

Our burdens have been lifted!

Praise His name!

Be joyful!

Smile!

HELEN WIDGER MIDDLEBROOKE
To Love and to Cherish

God Speaks

How sweet are your words to my taste,
sweeter than honey to my mouth!
I gain understanding from your precepts;
therefore I hate every wrong path.
Your word is a lamp for my feet,
a light on my path.

PSALM 119:103–105 NIV

After trying for two years to find a publisher for my first book, I desperately needed to hear from God. With tears of frustration, I cried out to Him, "When will all my labor pay off?" He responded through Jeremiah 31:16 (NIV), "'Restrain your voice from weeping and your eyes from tears, for your work will be rewarded,' declares the LORD."

He really heard my cry! And the reward He

promised? *Lambs on the Ledge* is now published not only in English, but in Portuguese, Chinese, and Russian, and is being read by pastors and leaders around the world. God is in the midst of every part of your life and mine. He is in the midst of every exciting and fruitful season—but He is also in the midst of the winters when all seems dead and still. He's there as only a best friend can be. And God will speak to us. He will speak through a million images and events around us and through His Word.

As we walk with God, we will be refreshed as we worship, and our souls will be fed as we study His Word. Prayer will become a natural two-way conversation that will give deep direction to our lives.

And God will not disappoint us!

JOYCE STRONG
Author, Speaker

There's Beauty in Humility

When the turn came for Esther. . .
to go to the king, she asked for nothing other
than what Hegai, the king's eunuch who was
in charge of the harem, suggested.
And Esther won the favor of
everyone who saw her.
ESTHER 2:15 NIV

Imagine a simple Jewish girl, a captive in Persia, being considered for the position of queen. Esther knew nothing of palace life in a strange land or how to please King Xerxes, who held her future in his hands. Humbly, she recognized her need to rely on others for wisdom. So Esther looked to the king's harem eunuch, Hegai, for advice. Hegai must have responded to Esther wisely, because she not only received the favor of all who saw her, she won the heart of the king.

No matter what your age or position, at times, you need advice. Like Esther, do you choose your counselors wisely? Then do you follow their good advice, or does pride get in the way?

Humility often requires courage. We assume people will think poorly of us if we admit we don't know all the facts or the best way to proceed. But often just the opposite is true. Humility has an appeal all its own. Remember, too, people may undervalue this gentle opinion-making quality, but God never will. Perhaps that's why He so often blesses the humble.

Humility doesn't come easily to me, Lord. Help me turn aside from pride and be meek instead.

PAMELA L. McQUADE
Daily Wisdom for the Workplace

Failure Misconception

His divine power has given us everything
we need for a godly life through our
knowledge of him who called us
by his own glory and goodness.
2 PETER 1:3 NIV

It is easy to think that one failure marks our identity as a failure. That is what the enemy wants us to believe. If he can make us feel as though we *are* a failure, then he's the winner.

Failure is just part of life, and the sooner we accept that we are flawed humans who depend on the perfect Christ, the sooner we put the taskmaster of perfection away.

What is failure anyway, except a man-made yardstick for performance? God is much more interested in the process than the product. If I obey God and lose the sale, I am still a success in God's eyes.

Perhaps it is not failure of a spiritual nature that has you bound. Perhaps it's failure of a marriage, of a job, of simple tasks that have influenced the perception that you are a failure. If so, consider this:

One basketball player missed nine thousand shots in his career. He lost more than three hundred games. Twenty-six times he was trusted to take the game's winning shot and missed. His name is Michael Jordan. He said, "I've failed over and over again in my life. And that's why I succeed."

We need to reject the lie of the enemy who tries to kick us when we are down by telling us the lie. Failure can be the springboard for future success.

SHARON JAYNES
*"I'm Not Good Enough". . .
and Other Lies Women Tell Themselves*

Outrageously Convinced

"Write down the revelation and make it plain on tablets so that a herald may run with it. For the revelation awaits an appointed time; it speaks of the end and will not prove false. Though it linger, wait for it; it will certainly come and will not delay."

HABAKKUK 2:2–3 NIV

Deborah is one of my heroes. At a time when the nation of Israel had strayed far from the worship of Jehovah and had been taken into captivity by the Canaanites, God raised up Deborah as a prophet and judge over the nation. Over the period of her rule, the Israelites gained their freedom as this courageous woman made wise decisions and led them into battle. What was the result? The entire land had peace for forty years. Deborah fulfilled her destiny because she followed God with faith and confidence.

We are all needed to make a holy difference in this world. In fact, God has chosen us to do just that (John 15:16). God asks you and me to be outrageously convinced that the purpose of our time here on earth is truly significant. . .so convinced that we will not give up the pursuit of the spiritual dreams He has placed in our hearts.

If God is giving you a dream for your life, write the vision down. Describe it. You'll never do what you cannot visualize. Then let God calculate the route and the timing. When He says to move, step out by faith and continue until you reach your destination. He will fulfill the plans He has for you! Trust Him.

JOYCE STRONG
Author, Speaker

Looking Ahead to Where God Is

But Jesus told him, "Anyone who puts a hand to the plow and then looks back is not fit for the Kingdom of God."
LUKE 9:62 NLT

We know that we shouldn't worry about tomorrow, but even worse is to worry and feel regret about the past, which can only cripple us for tomorrow. "I wish things could be the way they were." "I wish I were younger." "I wish my husband treated me like he did when we first met." "I wish I could fit into those jeans again. . . ." "I wish, I wish, I wish."

Although the Lord doesn't want us looking back at what once was, our enemy does. He wants us to feel discouraged and helpless over what we face today and drown in self-pity about how it was in the past. But God wants us to look ahead to the future. The future is where He is. He promises to give us hope in our futures. Let's claim that promise for ourselves, for our spouses, and for our marriages. Let's forget the past—it's long gone already and cannot be changed. Let's move ahead and press toward the new things that the Lord wants to do in our lives.

NICOLE O'DELL
To Love and to Cherish

For Us Who Believe

I pray that the eyes of your heart may be enlightened in order that you may know the hope to which he has called you, the riches of his glorious inheritance in his holy people, and his incomparably great power for us who believe.
EPHESIANS 1:18–19 NIV

No matter what you're facing today—no matter what giants are standing in your path—if God gives you the vision, He will give you the provision. He doesn't necessarily call the equipped, but He always equips the called. You have what it takes. God has given you the power of the Holy Spirit. That same power is what transformed Peter from a coward who denied he even knew Jesus into a courageous leader who spoke out with confidence and passion after Jesus' ascension.

Satan wants us to believe that we don't have

what it takes. God's truth is that we have everything we need. The power of the Holy Spirit has been given to us, is living in us, and is working through us. But here's the key. That power is *for those who believe* (Ephesians 1:18–20). The power is available, but we must believe to receive.

Satan tells me, "You can't."

God tells me, "I already have."

The only obstacle keeping us from doing all that God has called us to do and being all that God has called us to be is our unbelief. It was the same with the Israelites headed to the Promised Land, and it's the same for you and me headed to ours. Jesus said, "All things are possible to those who believe."

SHARON JAYNES
*"I'm Not Good Enough"...
and Other Lies Women Tell Themselves*

Joy in the Morning

The LORD is close to the brokenhearted and saves those who are crushed in spirit.
PSALM 34:18 NIV

Joy, a mother of three, struggled silently with her pains of loneliness and discouragement. No one really knew how desperate she felt. When she risked sharing, it was generally met with an endearing soul trying to assure her, "It will get better." But the truth was she was barely holding on—trying to make it through another day, another restless night.

She was waiting for things to change, waiting for someone to come to her aid or the dawn of a new day that would bring a new reality. She was tired of hopes and dreams. She had been there and done that, but the grim realities remained. Her life was mundane and full of recurring hurts from careless words, lack of appreciation, and unfulfilled dreams. Her energy was gone. She was putting on a mask, welcoming everyone with a cheerful hello and smile. Hope was gone. She felt overwhelmed, underappreciated, and extremely unhappy.

It is easy to become self-absorbed when life isn't going the way you want. It is also easy to judge others for not understanding, not being there for you, or not being able to "fix" your problem.

He is close to the brokenhearted, those who are at the end of their rope. He offers understanding that has no limits, healing for every wound, and mighty power to enable you to stand firm through the tough time until once again your heart can experience joy in the morning and throughout your day.

BOBBIE RILL
Family Life Radio Network

No Outlet

Commit thy way unto the LORD; trust also in him; and he shall bring it to pass.
PSALM 37:5 KJV

We can learn to *live* with difficult circumstances. Grace has the power to turn a seeming dead end into a new beginning, one that sets us on the path to life without end, amen. It is in that divine moment when grace breaks through the impossible situation and sets us emotionally free that we grow in our love for God. The reality of eternity is painted against the backdrop of our broken, hurting lives.

Sometimes, while traveling on life's journey, we get stopped by a bad attitude or sin, which can cripple us. We must first pull over and admit that something in our lives needs to change. Then we must jack the wheel off the ground and lift that situation to God in prayer. After that,

we must remove the flat tire and replace it with a new one, substituting the wrong attitude with a positive one.

When we make a commitment to fill our hearts with thoughts of His grace and power, the breath of God can inflate our flattened view of life. The word *encourage* means "to fill the heart." Encouragement can actually inflate a deflated attitude because it fills us with hope.

What is hope? It is the conviction that, despite all the black around you, despite the fact that you see no sign of an exit, you will find a way out—with God's help.

BARBARA JOHNSON
The Joyful Journey

Acting in Love

"I—yes, I alone—will blot out your sins
for my own sake and will never
think of them again."
Isaiah 43:25 NLT

Our awe-inspiring God demands perfection, and we so rarely give Him anything barely resembling it. When we look at our own imperfection, it's easy to become discouraged. Can we ever hit the mark? When we feel that way, we're much like a child who has disappointed Father. We respond with fear, doubt, or even resentment because we've made a mistake or intentionally disobeyed.

Before negative emotion gains ground in our lives, we must realize that God never loves us because we act perfectly any more than we want to give our children that kind of conditional love. God blots out sin not because of our character, but because of His. He wants to love us so badly that even sending Jesus to die for us was not too great a price.

Discouraged by your own sinfulness? Don't give up—give it to God. He'll forgive your past wrongs and forget them all as He gives you strength for new life in Him.

Forgive me, Lord, the wrongs I've done and the attitudes that do not glorify You. Change my heart and soul and make me whole in You.

PAMELA L. MCQUADE
Daily Wisdom for the Workplace

Worry or Worship

"Therefore do not worry about tomorrow,
for tomorrow will worry about its own things.
Sufficient for the day is its own trouble."
MATTHEW 6:34 NKJV

*I*t is when we find ourselves in these hard places that we make the choice to worry or worship. When we worry, we feel we have to come up with justifications and careful explanations for the naysayers. When we worry, we listen to the voices of Acceptance and Rejection. When we worry, we lay awake at night and ponder Satan's lies. When we worry, we have pity parties where the guests of honor are Negative Thinking, Doubt, and Resignation.

But we can make the choice to worship. When we worship in these hard places, we are reminded that none of this is about us—it is all about God. We turn our focus off of ourselves and back onto God Almighty. God can use empty places in your life to draw your heart to Him. He is the great love of your life who will never disappoint. He is building your eternal home that will never get broken, dirty, or need redecorating. He is preparing a place of eternal perfect fellowship.

We all worship something. We must choose whom—or what—we will worship. Will it be the opinions of others, our fears, or even our own comfort? Or will it be the One who created our souls to worship? Whatever we worship, we will obey. As we choose to be radically obedient to the Lord, we must be radical about choosing to worship Him and Him alone.

LYSA TERKEURST
Radically Obedient, Radically Blessed

The River

Consider it pure joy. . .whenever you face
trials of many kinds.
JAMES 1:2 NIV

Finding joy in the trials of life is like finding
a precious stone embedded along a river's edge.
As the water rages on, it is almost impossible
to spot the stone's vibrant colors, but when the
water is still, it is easy to see how it's been there
all along. These are deep lessons that, when
gathered together, strengthen our faith.

Turning away from trials is our natural
response to life, but if we remember the river
and the treasures that await us, they become
easier to bear. Jesus tells us that throughout life
we will have many troubles. At the same time,
He offers us strength by reminding us that He
has overcome them all (John 16:33). This is
of great comfort to us when life becomes the

raging river, and we struggle just to keep our head above the water.

In time, as the water of our days ebbs and flows, eventually the turbulence passes. We gasp and cough and cling to shore to find we survived, not only the current that threatened to pull us under, but our own doubt as well. And blinking to us in the sunlight, caught along the riverbank, are pearls of wisdom and a jewel called hope.

SARAH HAWKINS
To Love and to Cherish

Sincere Faith

But we have this treasure in jars of clay to show that this all-surpassing power is from God and not from us.

2 Corinthians 4:7 niv

I firmly believe the world doesn't need to see how perfect we are; it needs to see how powerful God is. People don't need to see how Christians never have any problems and never make any mistakes; they need to see how God is bigger than our problems and more powerful than our mistakes.

Another of my favorite passages is 2 Corinthians 2:17 (niv): "Unlike so many, we do not peddle the word of God for profit. On the contrary, in Christ we speak before God with sincerity, as those sent from God."

In the original Greek, the word *sincerity*, or sincere faith, literally means "without wax." During New Testament times, clay pots were big business. They were like first-century Tupperware—used for hauling and storing everything imaginable. Each jar of clay was handmade, and it was inevitable that there would be some kind of crack or flaw somewhere in it. Everyone knew about the cracks. But since it was big business, the people selling the clay pots would cover the cracks with wax. It was all a game.

In the same way, we have this treasure—the radiance and glory of the living God—but we have it in a jar of clay. Each of us is handmade by God, completely unique. But since we live in a fallen world, where our fellow jars of clay routinely bump into us, some cracks are inevitable.

DONNA PARTOW
This Isn't the Life I Signed Up For

Just as You Are

"But while he was still a long way off,
his father saw him and was filled with
compassion for him; he ran to his son,
threw his arms around him and kissed him."
LUKE 15:20 NIV

As we went around the table, I listened to
the women each share who they were, what
they did, and some struggles they face in their
job. I knew immediately I did not belong. After
I took my turn, I had every woman looking
at me as if I had four ears growing out of my
head. There was an awkward silence, and then
we moved on to the next lady. The catch phrase
"Wanna get away?" echoed in my mind.

Scripture continually paints God as our
Father who wants us to come to Him as we are.
He doesn't want us to pretend we are someone
we are not. He doesn't expect us or require us

to have it all together. Jesus called disciples who were not considered "smart" enough by Jewish teachers to follow and learn from Him. He beckoned others who were hated and treated as outcasts. He showed love and gave value to women who in society's eyes deserved to die. His ancestors consisted of the righteous and sinners alike—adulterers, prostitutes, and those from dysfunctional families. Jesus wants us as we are—despite our past mistakes, present struggles, or fears for the future. He wants us no matter how long we have been away. He is waiting with arms open wide. God wants us to come to Him, to be a part of His family.

JOCELYN HAMSHER
Circle of Friends

Don't Miss It!

And we know that in all things God works for
the good of those who love him,
who have been called according to his purpose.
ROMANS 8:28 NIV

That good could be knowing God more intimately, being conformed to the image of Christ more completely, understanding the scriptures more clearly, communing with the Spirit more intimately, falling in love with Him more dearly. God often allows or orchestrates certain circumstances in our lives in order to draw us into dependency on Him and intimacy with Him.

All day long God is working in and around us. It is so easy to simply go about the task of living without seeing God's handprints on our circumstances and footprints on our paths. When we see life as a to-do list to check off or random acts of fortune to celebrate or misfortune to endure, we will miss seeing God and hearing His voice as the scarlet thread that connects the moments and the days of our lives.

It is so easy to miss God speaking through our circumstances. Jesus' first miracle occurred at a wedding in Cana. Some noticed the miracle and some did not. Sometimes God speaks to us in very unlikely ways, and if we're not looking for it, we may miss it. Being in tune with His voice requires more than our ears to hear and our eyes to see. Oh, how I never want to miss God working through my circumstances as I travel through life!

SHARON JAYNES
Becoming a Woman Who Listens to God

Guidance

*"I'll take the hand of those who don't know
the way, who can't see where they're going.
I'll be a personal guide to them,
directing them through unknown country.
I'll be right there to show them what roads to
take, make sure they don't fall into the ditch.
These are the things I'll be doing for them—
sticking with them, not leaving
them for a minute."*

Isaiah 42:16 MSG

The guidance of the Spirit is generally by
gentle suggestions or drawings, not in violent
pushes; it requires great childlikeness of heart to
be faithful to it. The secret of being made willing lies in a definite giving up of our will.

You must lay this burden about any service
to which you may be called wholly upon your
burden bearer. If He wants you to do it, He will

supply all the needed strength and wisdom, and you don't even have to think of it or worry about it for one single moment. Only see to it that you yield yourself up to Him perfectly, and then leave it with Him. There never must be any indulgence in an unsurrendered will in any respect, for this would bring darkness at once.

Now you must claim continually that it is true. When it seems to be the most untrue, then claim and assert it with the greatest boldness. This is what it means to lift up the shield of faith, and this is the way to overcome by faith. It is marvelous to see what He can do with even the poorest and the weakest instruments that are pliable in His hands!

HANNAH WHITALL SMITH
The Christian's Secret of a Holy Life

The World's First GPS System

Then the angel of God, who had been traveling in front of Israel's army, withdrew and went behind them. The pillar of cloud also moved from in front and stood behind them, coming between the armies of Egypt and Israel. Throughout the night the cloud brought darkness to the one side and light to the other side; so neither went near the other all night long.

Exodus 14:19–20 niv

The world's first known GPS system was the pillar of cloud by day or fire by night that led the Israelites through the Sinai Peninsula. Imagine how comforting it was for the Israelites to follow that pillar on their trek. Better than a road map! It was a visible symbol, concrete evidence, of the presence of God.

Imagine if we had that holy pillar outside of our front door to help us with big decisions: *Lord, should we take that job and move to another state? Or should we just stay put?*

We do have that holy pillar outside of our homes. Inside, too. The Bible! Searching God's Word is like choosing to follow a map in a new country. He shows us where we need to end up and how we need to get there. Like God's people crossing the barren Sinai desert, the Bible teaches us to listen for God's directions, whether it's "Stop!" or "Camp here tonight" or "Quick, get a move on!" or "Time to rest." God's voice in our ear is the only map we need.

Suzanne Woods Fisher
To Love and to Cherish

Righteousness for Ragamuffins

*For He made Him who knew no sin to be sin
for us, that we might become the
righteousness of God in Him.*
2 Corinthians 5:21 NKJV

My smart but spacey friend enthused in a
strong Southern twang, "You know, I think
the Gospel is kind of like the Cinderella story.
Christians are like Cinderella and Jesus is like
the prince."

After mulling it over for a while, I realized
the reason I had such a strong aversion to the
analogy was because Cinderella *deserved* the
prince. If you've read the book or watched the
DVD, you probably remember that Cinderella
was beautiful. She was also a friend of animals
and had an admirable work ethic. So when the

slipper fits and the prince confesses his crush, most of us sigh dreamily, grateful for the happy ending—glad the good girl ends up with the good guy.

That is so *not* the Gospel.

In *God's story*, the prince falls head over heels in love with the ugly stepsister—the one with moles on her face, frizzy hair, a whiny personality, and elastic-waist pants. She isn't pretty, inside or out. The whole ballroom lets out a collective gasp when the handsome prince strides across the floor and asks her to dance. His choice in partners doesn't make sense. She doesn't *deserve* His affection, or anyone else's for that matter.

Then something amazing happens: as she's enveloped in the prince's adoring embrace, the stepsister *becomes* beautiful.

That's the Gospel.

LISA HARPER
What the Bible Is All About for Women

Confidence to Serve Well

*[Deborah] held court under the Palm of
Deborah. . .and the Israelites went up to
her to have their disputes decided.*
JUDGES 4:5 NIV

What an unusual person Deborah was!
Judges were usually men, yet she held this
position of importance, deciding major issues
for the people of Israel. In a time when most
people thought of women as being fairly
unimportant, she held a powerful position and
seems to have been a good leader.

Like Deborah, we can find ourselves in
unusual jobs. Perhaps you're the only person
of your sex on your job. Maybe you are young,
working with people greatly senior to you. Or
perhaps you are the only person of your race on
the job. Being the one who's different can be a
challenge. Your position can be one to complain

about or one to learn from. The scriptures don't show Deborah whining or complaining. She took charge of the situation. She did her best for God, and an impressive best it was.

Whether you fit in completely or find yourself in a tough spot, you're there to serve God, not complain or quit easily. So make even your differences work for God, no matter what they are.

I may feel different, Lord, but You've given me this place. Let me serve You by doing my best every day.

PAMELA L. MCQUADE
Daily Wisdom for the Workplace

Eternal Perspective

Simon Peter answered him, "Lord, who would we go to? You have the words that give eternal life. We believe and know that you are the Holy One from God."
JOHN 6:68–69 NCV

The account in John 6 says that people were following Jesus. The contrasts in that crowd tell the whole story. They were seeking a circus. Jesus was offering truth. They demanded outward drama. Jesus sought inward change. They looked for a hero. Jesus came to be a servant. When they did not get what they wanted, many of those brand-new disciples packed up their marbles and went home.

Peter went on to deny Jesus three times—but over time his early conviction took root.

If we look closely, Peter gives us the secret of an eternal perspective. He reminds us of two important builders: (1) our hope rests in the power of Christ's resurrection; (2) our hope is fixed on the promise of our reward.

No matter what life dishes out along the way, there is nowhere to go but to Christ. Peter's entire challenge to people in pain involved reminding them they were pilgrims—people who were just passing through this fallen world. Then he helped them focus on "goin' home."

Think of it. One day doubts and fears will all be in the past. We will be in a kingdom that cannot be shaken. No more unanswerable questions. No more unexplainable suffering. No more riveting doubts. No more paralyzing fear. We will see Him as He is. As we look at the nail prints, we will finally understand.

CAROL KENT
Tame Your Fears

Call on My Name

"They will call on my name and I will answer them; I will say, 'They are my people,' and they will say, 'The LORD is our God.'"

ZECHARIAH 13:9 NIV

One of the reasons we do not have the wholeness, fulfillment, and peace we desire is that we have not acknowledged God as the answer to our every need. We think, *He may have given me eternal life, but I don't know if He can handle my financial problems.* Or we think, *I know He can lead me to a better job, but I'm not sure if He can mend this marriage.* Or, *He healed my back, but I don't know if He can take away my depression.* The truth is, He is *everything* we need, and we have to remember that always. In fact, it's good to tell yourself daily, "God is everything I need," and then say the name of the Lord that answers your specific need at that moment.

Do you need hope? He is called our Hope. Pray, "Jesus, You are my Hope."

Are you weak? He is called our Strength. Pray, "Jesus, You are my Strength."

Do you need advice? He is called Counselor. Pray, "Jesus, You are my Counselor."

Do you feel oppressed? He is called Deliverer.

Are you lonely? He is called Companion and Friend.

He is also called Emmanuel, which means "God with us." He is not some distant, cold being with no interest in you. He is Emmanuel, the God who is with you right now to the degree that you acknowledge Him in your life.

STORMIE OMARTIAN
Praying God's Will for Your Life

What Does God See?

*Since you were precious in My sight, you have
been honored, and I have loved you.*

Isaiah 43:4 NKJV

If you are disappointed in yourself, you
assume God is, too. If your parents discovered
when they visited you in college that you
had a beer in your fridge and were verbally
disappointed, didn't you think God felt that
way, too? If you missed a few Sundays at church
and bumped into someone in a coffee shop
who commented on your absence, didn't you
also feel you had let God down? If your child's
lowest grade at school was Bible class, didn't you
wonder what you had done wrong as a parent
and if God considered you a dunderhead? The
negatives we receive from others we project
onto God, and we walk through our lives

thinking we have let Him down and He is very disappointed.

The fact is we're wrong. Jesus told us flat out that's not how our Father thinks. The Gospels are full of stories of Jesus taking the morality of the day and turning it on its head. Jesus never minimized sin, but He separated the sinner from the sin that had a hold on her. This means He might not like what you do, but He absolutely, unconditionally adores you yourself.

SHEILA WALSH
Let Go

God of Hope

I pray that God, the source of hope,
will fill you completely with joy and peace
because you trust in him. Then you will
overflow with confident hope through
the power of the Holy Spirit.
ROMANS 15:13 NLT

In our busy, fast-paced lives, we may feel exhausted at times. Our culture fosters frenzy and ignores the need for rest and restoration. Constantly putting out fires and completing tasks, working incessantly, we may feel discouraged and disheartened with life. There is more to life than this, isn't there?

Our God of hope says, "Yes!" God desires to fill us to the brim with joy and peace. But to receive this gladness, rest, and tranquillity, we need to have faith in the God who is trustworthy and who says, "Anything is possible if a person believes" (Mark 9:23 NLT). We need to place our confidence in God who, in His timing and through us, will complete that task, mend that relationship, or do whatever it is we need. The key to receiving and living a life of hope, joy, and peace is recounting God's faithfulness out loud, quietly in your heart, and to others. When you begin to feel discouraged, exhausted, and at the end of your rope, stop; go before the throne of grace and recall God's faithfulness.

TINA C. ELACQUA
Whispers of Wisdom for Busy Women

Gomer, a Picture of Israel

The LORD said to Hosea, "Go, take to yourself a wife of harlotry and have children of harlotry; for the land commits flagrant harlotry, forsaking the LORD." So he went and took Gomer the daughter of Diblaim, and she conceived and bore him a son.

HOSEA 1:2–3 NASB

Do you have a child who has wandered away from every good thing you tried to give him? Your heart has broken as that child perhaps chose a lifestyle that so contradicted your own. Now imagine God going through this same kind of pain as an entire nation, one He dearly loved, refused to walk with Him.

Why would God ask the prophet Hosea to enter into an unwholesome alliance? Because He wanted Israel to understand what it was like to observe the one to whom they were betrothed go off and play the harlot. When Israel entered into the covenant with God, the people had promised fidelity to Him. But this beloved nation had "prostituted" themselves in worship of false gods, forsaking their true God.

The book of Hosea reveals the brokenness of God's own heart as He watched Israel wander away. Now God was forced to take action against the people He loved in order to bring them back to Him.

CAROL L. FITZPATRICK
Daily Wisdom for Women

Going through the Fire

*So Shadrach, Meshach, and Abednego
stepped out of the fire. Then the high officers,
officials, governors, and advisers crowded
around them and saw that the fire had not
touched them. Not a hair on their heads was
singed, and their clothing was not scorched.
They didn't even smell of smoke!*
DANIEL 3:26–27 NLT

There is a saying when we're going through
something really tough—that we're going
through the fire.

It's just a metaphor of course, but it sure
describes the feeling, doesn't it? I know of so
many people lately—dealing with health issues
. . .the death of a loved one. . .job loss. . .marital
trouble—so many people going through the
fire.

And it makes me think of those three

young men—Shadrach, Meshach, and Abed-nego—who went through real fire.

The thing that has always impressed me about that story is that they were thrown into the fire bound, but when they came back out again, only one thing had burned: not their clothes, skin, or hair. No—the only thing that had been burned in the furnace was that which had bound them. They came out *unbound*!

We wonder why the Lord allows us to go through the fire—maybe it's only to destroy that thing that has us bound, too.

SUZIE THOMAS
Circle of Friends

Go Forth and Produce

May the favor of the Lord our God rest on us;
establish the work of our hands for us.
PSALM 90:17 NIV

As sons and daughters of God, we are called to imitate Christ (that is what the word *Christian* means—"Christ-follower") and continue the work of God on earth. We are to finish what He started, which is to be fruitful and productive in whatever field we find ourselves in.

As you strive to complete the work placed in your hands, you should find delight and fulfillment in it. If you are an administrator, you should be thriving on the details of your work, flourishing as you supervise others with grace and authority. If you are an artist, your creativity—the things God has placed within you to express—should surprise you!

No matter what your profession, it should

reveal your strengths to you—as well as your weaknesses, the areas that could use improvement and refining. All of this is how we bless others and glorify God as we grow into a greater reflection of His creative power. Understanding that we are literally the extension of God's arms to the world is huge. Our inherent talents or gifts actually make up the expression of His care for those on earth.

MICHELLE MCKINNEY HAMMOND
How to Make Life Work

Futile Faith?

"My righteous ones will live by faith.
But I will take no pleasure in
anyone who turns away."
HEBREWS 10:38 NLT

We clean the windows and wash the car, and a day later it rains. We sweep the kitchen floor, and hours later the crunch of cookie crumbs resounds under our feet. Some tasks seem so futile.

So it is with our spiritual life. We pray unceasingly and no answers seem to come, or we work tirelessly and problems entrench us. In frustration we wonder, *Why did this happen? What purpose is there to all of this?* It all seems so pointless.

To the skeptic, logic must pervade every situation. If not, there is no basis for belief. But to the person of faith, logic gives way to

faith—especially during the most tumultuous, nonsensical times.

So even when our prayers remain unanswered, we continue to pray. Even when God is silent, we continue to believe. And though we grope for answers, we continue to trust.

When our chaotic lives turn upside down and we labor to find rhyme and reason, God asks us to hold fast to our faith. For no labor of love is pointless; no prayer is futile.

TINA KRAUSE
Whispers of Wisdom for Busy Women

God Loves You—
Flaws and All

So let's come near God with pure hearts and a
confidence that comes from having faith.
HEBREWS 10:22 CEV

If you listen closely, you can hear them.
Women around the globe, groaning and moan-
ing in dressing rooms. Are they in pain? Are
they ill? No, it's just bathing suit season, and
they're trying to find the one perfect suit that
doesn't make them look fat. It's a quest every
woman embarks on, and it's one of the most
daunting tasks she will ever face.

Seriously, is there anything more humbling
than standing in front of a dressing room
mirror, under those unforgiving fluorescent
lights, trying on bathing suit after bathing suit?
While you might be able to hide a few dimples

underneath blue jeans or a nice black dress, you're not hiding anything in a bathing suit.

That's pretty much how it is with God. You might be able to fake grin your way through church. But when you enter the throne room, it's like wearing your bathing suit before God. You can't hide any imperfections from Him.

Here's the great thing about God. He gave us Jesus to take care of our sin, because God knew we'd be flawed. We can't earn our way into God's favor. All we have to do is ask Jesus to be the Lord of our lives, and we're "in." Then, whenever we enter the throne room, God sees us through "the Jesus filter," and all He sees is perfection. Now if we could just figure out some kind of perfection filter for bathing suit season, life would be super.

MICHELLE MEDLOCK ADAMS
Secrets of Beauty

The Power of Unity

Now the multitude of those who believed were of one heart and one soul. . . .
And with great power the apostles gave witness to the resurrection of the Lord Jesus.
And great grace was upon them all.
ACTS 4:32-33 NKJV

The ultimate power of prayer is found in a church where people of one mind unite.

The need to come together is an integral part of our makeup. In Genesis we read, "The LORD God said, It is not good that the man should be alone" (2:18 KJV). We were *created* to come together before God. When Jesus taught us how to pray, He didn't begin with "*My* Father which art in heaven" but "*Our* Father which art in heaven."

The evidence of the power of gathering and praying in one accord is staggering! And it's not only the *power* felt amid Christ's presence, but the *joy* of a holy fellowship!

The church is where the Word of God is taught, spiritual direction gleaned, and encouragement given. The body of Christ is a living body that serves a living God. And it is a place of power only when we are united, seeking and moving together in *His* will.

The church is the place where we are all reminded of the power of unity under God. It is where our focus is to be solely on the heavens above, a place where we gather with one common purpose—to love God and each other. In such a spiritual haven, fellow believers are pulled away from earthly concerns and look to Christ seated in the heavenlies with God. There is no greater joy!

DONNA K. MALTESE
Power Prayers to Start Your Day

Holding On

*We should remove from our lives anything
that would get in the way and the sin
that so easily holds us back.*

HEBREWS 12:1 NCV

I saw a television show that both fascinated
and repelled me. It was about hoarders; that is,
people who are unable to throw anything away.
I found out that it's not that they *want* to live
this way—they are unable to force themselves to
make decisions and things just pile up on them,
literally.

One dear man could not get the door to his
one-room efficiency apartment shut. In another
lady's house her "stuff" had piled up to shoulder
height *in every room*! Eventually she was simply
overwhelmed by the enormous task of deciding
what to keep and what to throw away.

It made me pause to wonder if I'm not

more like these precious people than I would like to admit. Am I hoarding things in my spiritual life—holding on to shattered dreams and unfulfilled plans, unable to let go of old hurts and wounds, salvaging every scrap of disappointment or heartache, or piling up justifications for my attitude and responses to other people? Have I let the mess of my sins drop on the floor of my life, afraid to let go or allow God to have full rein and clean me up?

As with the people who sought out help to clean up their homes, it is a process that takes the support of someone with the ability to help untangle the mess. Spiritually speaking, that's our Helper, the Holy Spirit.

MISSY HORSFALL
Circle of Friends

The Will to Fulfill

And there we saw the giants, the sons of
Anak, which come of the giants:
and we were in our own sight as grasshoppers,
and so we were in their sight.
NUMBERS 13:33 KJV

The ten fearful spies who joined Caleb on the trip into Canaan may have had what we'd call a poor self-image. Compared to the Canaanites, they seemed to be small potatoes—grasshoppers even! And they imagined that their enemies would see them as these irritating insects. When the Israelite spies described themselves that way, they were relying on their own power. And looking at it from that perspective, they were probably right. They didn't have the ability to overthrow people who had cities and villages in Canaan. The Canaanites were entrenched in the land, and moving them out was a big project.

Unlike Caleb and Joshua, these men didn't consider doing the job under God's power. They forgot who had led them there and what He'd promised them.

When you feel like a grasshopper compared to coworkers, huge projects, or anything else, are you looking at yourself through the right lens? Are you seeing your working life through God's eyes or your own?

Lord, lead me in my working life. I know You've brought me here for a reason, and I want to fulfill Your will.

PAMELA L. MCQUADE
Daily Wisdom for the Workplace

Persistence

"For the past twenty-three years. . .
the LORD has been giving me his messages.
I have faithfully passed them on to you."
JEREMIAH 25:3 NLT

The Bible is full of persistent people, people
who persevered despite problems and difficul-
ties, long after the time most people would
consider such persistence wise. Noah spent
one hundred years building the ark. Abraham
waited twenty-five years for Isaac, the son of
promise. And by the end of his life, Jeremiah
had preached God's message to an unbelieving
audience for forty years. Israelites called him
a traitor, threw him in prison, and left him to
die, but he continued preaching God's message.
Nothing slowed him down.

Jeremiah's faith enabled him to persevere.
The writer of Hebrews could have had Jeremiah

in mind when he wrote, "Some faced. . .chains and imprisonment. . . . They went about. . . destitute, persecuted and mistreated—the world was not worthy of them" (Hebrews 11:36–38 NIV).

God expects the same persistence of us. He calls for persistence, also known as perseverance, over a dozen times in the New Testament. He means for the trials that come our way to increase our perseverance. When we successfully pass small hurdles, He may put bigger ones in our way. Why? Because He doesn't love us? No—because He does.

Persistence results in faith that is pure, molten gold.

DARLENE FRANKLIN
Whispers of Wisdom for Busy Women

Title Index

Contributors

Michelle Medlock Adams has a diverse résumé featuring inspirational books, children's picture books, and greeting cards. Her insights have appeared in periodicals across America, including *Today's Christian Woman* and *Guideposts for Kids*. She lives in Fort Worth, Texas, with her husband, two daughters, and a "mini petting zoo."

Emily Biggers is a gifted education specialist in a north Texas public school district. She enjoys travel, freelance writing, and serving in a local apartment ministry through her church.

Joanna Bloss is a personal trainer, writer, and student living in the Midwest. She is a coauthor of *Grit for the Oyster: 250 Pearls of Wisdom for Aspiring Authors*.

Jill Briscoe is the author of more than forty books—including devotionals, study guides, poetry, and children's books. She serves as executive editor of *Just Between Us* magazine and served on the boards of World Relief and *Christianity Today* for more than twenty years. Jill and her husband make their home in Milwaukee, Wisconsin.

Amy Carmichael (1867–1951) was a Protestant Christian missionary in India who opened an orphanage and founded a mission in Dohnavur. She served in India for fifty-six years without furlough and authored many books about her missionary work.

Fanny Crosby (1820–1915), blinded in infancy, became one of the most popular and prolific of all hymn writers. She wrote more than eight thousand hymns in her lifetime, including the best-known "Blessed Assurance," "Jesus Is Tenderly Calling You Home," "Praise Him, Praise Him," and "To God Be the Glory."

Nancy Leigh DeMoss grew up in a family deeply committed to Christ and to the mission of world evangelization. Today, Nancy mentors millions of women through Revive Our Hearts and the True Woman Movement, calling them to heart revival and biblical womanhood. Her books have sold more than two million copies and include *Lies Women Believe* and *A Thirty-Day Walk with God in the Psalms.* She also coauthored *Seeking Him* and *Lies Young Women Believe* and is the general editor of *Becoming God's True Woman.*

Dena Dyer is a writer who resides in the Texas Hill Country. She has contributed to more than a dozen anthologies and has authored or coauthored three humor books. Find out more about Dena at www .denadyer.com.

Tina C. Elacqua teaches, writes, and publishes journal articles, books, conference papers and presentations, and technical reports/presentations. She has held roles of research scientist, professor, and consultant in industrial/organizational psychology.

Elisabeth Elliot is a bestselling author of more than twenty books including *Passion and Purity*, *Be Still My Soul*, *The Path of Loneliness*, and *Keep a Quiet Heart*. She and her husband, Lars Gren, make their home in Magnolia, Massachusetts.

Suzanne Woods Fisher's historical novels, *Copper Star* and its sequel, *Copper Fire*, are inspired by true events. Fisher writes for many magazines, is a wife and mother, and is a puppy raiser for Guide Dogs for the Blind.

Carol L. Fitzpatrick is a bestselling author of nine books that have totaled nearly three-quarters of a million books sold. She is a frequent conference speaker for writing groups and church groups. Carol and her husband have three grown children and three grandchildren. Although she credits her Midwest upbringing for instilling her core values, she has lived in California for nearly four decades.

Darlene Franklin lives in Englewood, Colorado. She is the author of several romance novels for Barbour's Heartsong Presents! series, as well as the Dressed for Death mystery series and numerous articles. You may visit her website at www.darlene hfranklin.com.

Michelle McKinney Hammond is a bestselling author, speaker, singer, and television cohost. She has authored more than thirty books, including the bestselling titles *The Diva Principle*; *Sassy, Single, and Satisfied*; *101 Ways to Get and Keep His Attention*; and *Secrets of an Irresistible Woman*. She makes her home in Chicago.

Jocelyn Hamsher is a gifted Bible study teacher, writer, board member, and speaker for Circle of Friends Ministries. She lives in Sugarcreek, Ohio, with her husband, Bruce, and their three sons. She enjoys spending time with family, studying the Word of God, drinking coffee, and laughing with her husband.

Janice Hanna, who lives in the Houston area, writes novels, nonfiction, magazine articles, and musical comedies for the stage. The mother of four married daughters, she is quickly adding grand-children to the family mix.

Lisa Harper is a communicator, author, speaker, and Bible teacher. She has spoken at Women of Faith, Moody Bible, Winsome Women, and Focus on the Family conferences and has written a number of books including *A Perfect Mess: How God Adores and Transforms Imperfect People Like Us*.

Frances Ridley Havergal (1836–1879) was an English poet and hymn writer. "Take My Life and Let It Be" is one of her best-known hymns. She also wrote hymn melodies, religious tracts, and works for children.

Sarah Hawkins is an English and Bible teacher to junior high students and has often taught a women's Bible study. She lives with her husband and son in Northern California.

Missy Horsfall is a published magazine and greeting card writer and coauthor of the novel *Love Me Back to Life*. A pastor's wife, she is a speaker and Bible study teacher for Circle of Friends and serves on the board overseeing its writing ministries. Missy also produces and cohosts the COF radio program.

Julie Hufstetler is a singer, songwriter, and worship leader who encourages and connects with listeners, whether she's singing alongside recording artist Mark Schultz or with noted speakers like Sheila Walsh, Dee Brestin, and Nancy Leigh DeMoss. She and her husband, Guy, live in northeast Ohio, with their three sons.

Sharon Jaynes is the author of thirteen books with Harvest House Publishers, Focus on the Family, and Moody Publishers and a frequent guest on national radio and television. She has also written numerous magazine articles and devotions for publications such as *Focus on the Family*, *Decision*, Crosswalk.com, and *In Touch*.

Barbara Johnson (1927–2007) was an award-winning author and Women of Faith Speaker Emeritus with more than four million books in print and translated into ten foreign languages. She faced her long battle with cancer with the same humor and wisdom with which she met the many adversities of her life.

Austine Keller resides in Tampa, Florida, writing and publishing as a ministry to others as well as for her own enjoyment. She also enjoys a newly emptied nest and fishing with her husband.

Carol Kent is an internationally known speaker and author. Her books include *When I Lay My Isaac Down*, *Becoming a Woman of Influence*, and *Mothers Have Angel Wings*. She is president of Speak Up Speaker Services and the founder and director of Speak Up with Confidence seminars.

Tina Krause is an award-winning newspaper columnist and author of the book *Laughter Therapy*. She is a wife, mom, and grandmother of four. Tina and her husband, Jim, live in Valparaiso, Indiana.

Donna K. Maltese is a freelance writer, editor, and proofreader; publicist for a local Mennonite project; and the assistant director of RevWriter Writers' Conferences. Donna resides in Bucks County, Pennsylvania, with her husband and two children. She is a pastor's prayer partner and is active in her local church.

Pamela L. McQuade is a freelance writer and editor in Nutley, New Jersey, who has worked with numerous publishers. Her Barbour credits include *The Word on Life*, *Daily Wisdom for Couples*, and *Prayers and Promises*, all coauthored with Toni Sortor. Pam and her husband share their home with basset hounds and are involved in basset hound rescue.

Helen Widger Middlebrooke is a homemaker, home educator, and mother of nine. She is a freelance columnist and the author of *Lessons for a Supermom* (Barbour Publishing, 2002).

Janine Miller grew up in Holmes County, Ohio. She currently homeschools her children, ages five to fifteen, and works part-time from her home as a church secretary. Janine and her husband of twenty-three years live in southern Ohio with their four children.

Mandy Nydegger lives with her husband, David, in Waco, Texas. She loves Christmas, snow, and the Indianapolis Colts.

Nicole O'Dell, wife and mother of three, is an accomplished writer of books, devotions, and Bible studies. She has been a Bible study leader and teacher for over fifteen years.

Stormie Omartian is a popular writer, speaker, and author. She is author of the bestselling The Power of Praying® books as well as many other titles. She and her husband have been married thirty years and have three grown children.

Donna Partow is an author and motivational speaker. Her books, including *This Isn't the Life I Signed Up For. . .But I'm Finding Hope and Healing* and *Becoming a Vessel God Can Use*, have sold almost a million copies, and her ministry Pieces4Peace reaches into the largest Muslim city in the world.

Elizabeth Prentiss (1818–1878) was the daughter of an early nineteenth-century revival preacher and began writing as a teenager. Born in 1818 in

Portland, Maine, Prentiss was also the writer of the hymn "More Love to Thee, O Christ." Prentiss died in Vermont in 1878.

Sarah Mae Ratliff enjoys worshipping God, writing, working with children, and spending time with her family. Sarah and her husband, Ryan, are high school sweethearts who welcomed their first son into the world last April.

Julie Rayburn is a public speaker and an area director for Community Bible Study. She lives in Atlanta with her husband, Scott. They have two grown children and one granddaughter.

Becki Reiser is wife to Jeff and mother to three grown boys and one daughter. After the murder of their seventeen-year-old daughter, Jeff and Becki began a ministry of sharing their testimony of forgiveness. Becki is a contributing author to Standard Publishing's *Devotions* magazine and the Circle of Friends website, www.circleoffriends.fm.

Ramona Richards is a freelance writer and editor living in Tennessee. Formerly the editor of *Ideals* magazine, Ramona has also edited children's books, fiction, nonfiction, study Bibles, and reference books for major Christian publishers. She is the author of *A Moment with God for Single Parents*.

Bobbie Rill is a motivational speaker and life coach. As a licensed professional counselor, she served as executive director over a multi-state network of Christian counseling and educational centers. She also directed Women of Virtue, a national conference and radio ministry. She and her husband, Bob, reside in Tucson, Arizona.

Frances J. Roberts (1918–2009) is best known for her classic devotional *Come Away My Beloved*. She founded the King's Press in 1964, where she authored and published *Come Away* and eight other books, selling over 1.5 million copies in the last thirty years.

Leah Slawson has been married to her husband, Guice, for more than twenty years and they have two teenagers, a son and daughter. She lives in Montgomery, Alabama.

Hannah Whitall Smith (1832–1911) was born into a strict Quaker home in Philadelphia and became a major influence in the Holiness movement of the late nineteenth century. Besides *The Christian's Secret of a Happy Life*, Smith also wrote *The God of All Comfort* and an autobiography, *The Unselfishness of God and How I Discovered It*.

Joyce Strong is an author and international conference speaker whose books include *Journey to Joy*; *Leading with Passion and Grace*; *Instruments for His Glory*; *Lambs on the Ledge*; *Caught in the Crossfire*; *Of Dreams and Kings and Mystical Things*; and *A Dragon, A Dreamer, and the Promise Giver*.

Corrie ten Boom (1892–1983) was simply an ordinary, middle-aged Dutch spinster when the Second World War began. By the time the conflict ended, she was literally transformed by the faith she had merely accepted and on a mission from God. By God's grace, Corrie survived the concentration camp and became a "tramp for the Lord," sharing in more than sixty nations the thrilling message that nothing, not even death, can separate us from God's love.

Lysa TerKeurst is a nationally known speaker and president of the Proverbs 31 Ministry. An award-winning author of twelve books, including *Becoming More Than a Good Bible Study Girl*, she has been featured on *Focus on the Family*, *Family Life Today*, *Good Morning America*, and in *Woman's Day* magazine.

Suzie Thomas serves Malone University as director of university relations and editor of *The Malone Magazine.* Author of *Read It Again Bible Stories: The Miracles of Jesus*, Suzie has a bachelor's degree in education and a master's in communication. She also has experience as a producer and radio host.

Sheila Walsh is a unique combination of international author, speaker, worship leader, television talk show host, and Bible teacher. She is a speaker with Women of Faith and the bestselling author of her memoir, *Honestly*, and the Gold Medallion Award nominee *The Heartache No One Sees*.

Permissions

Scripture Index

What Is Circle of Friends?

Circle of Friends Ministries, Inc., is a nonprofit organization established to build a pathway for women to come into a personal relationship with Jesus Christ and to build Christian unity among women. Our mission is to honor Jesus Christ through meeting the needs of women in our local, national, and international communities. Our vision is to be women who are committed to Jesus Christ, obediently seeking God's will and fulfilling our life mission as Christ followers. As individuals and as a corporate group, we minister a Christ-centered hope, biblically based encouragement, and unconditional love by offering God-honoring, Word-based teaching, worship, accountability, and fellowship to women in a nondenominational environment through speaker services,